Karin Offender

Have a question or concern? Let us know.

www.goodstore.me | info@goodstore.me | karinoffender@gmail.com

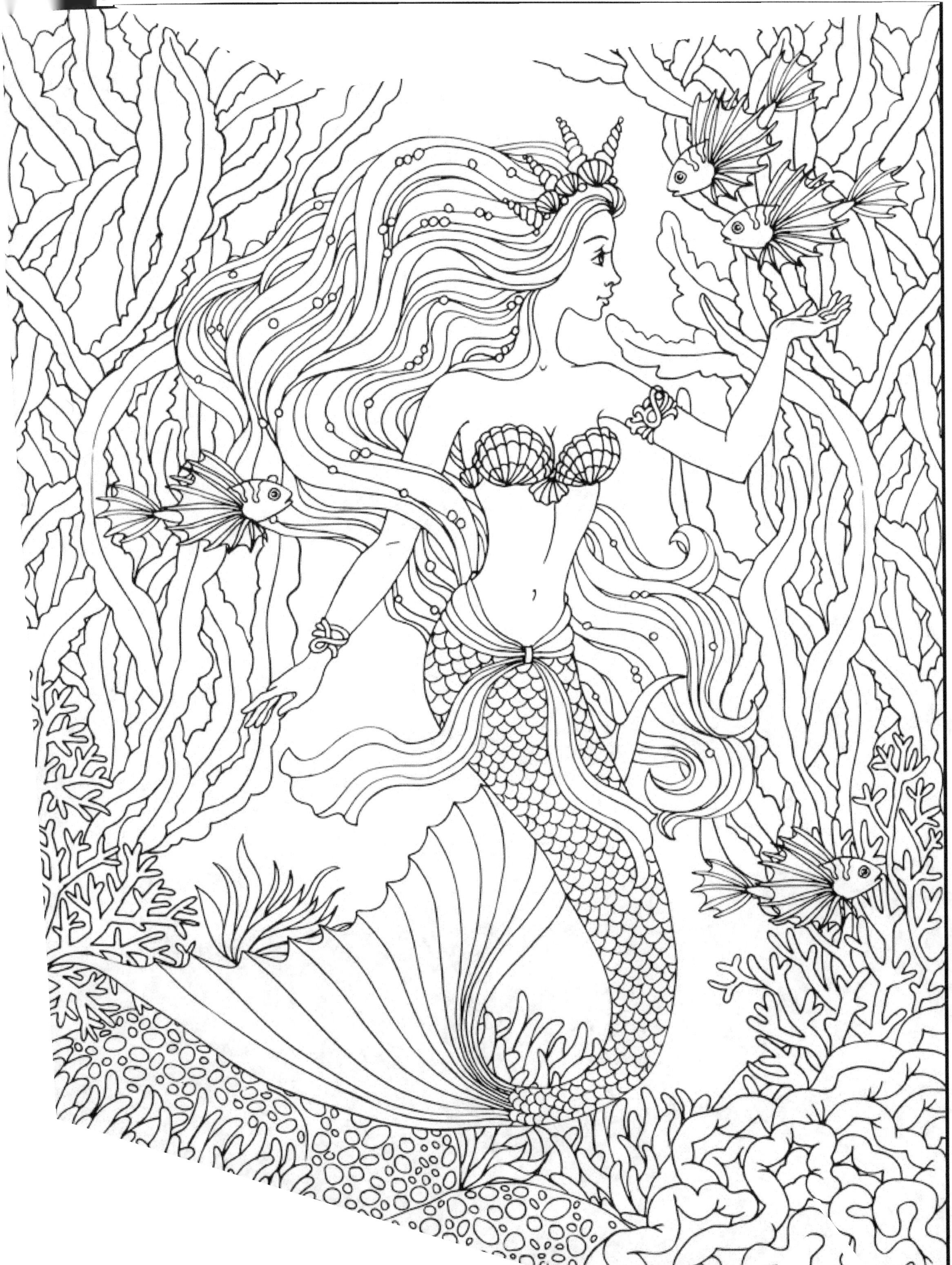

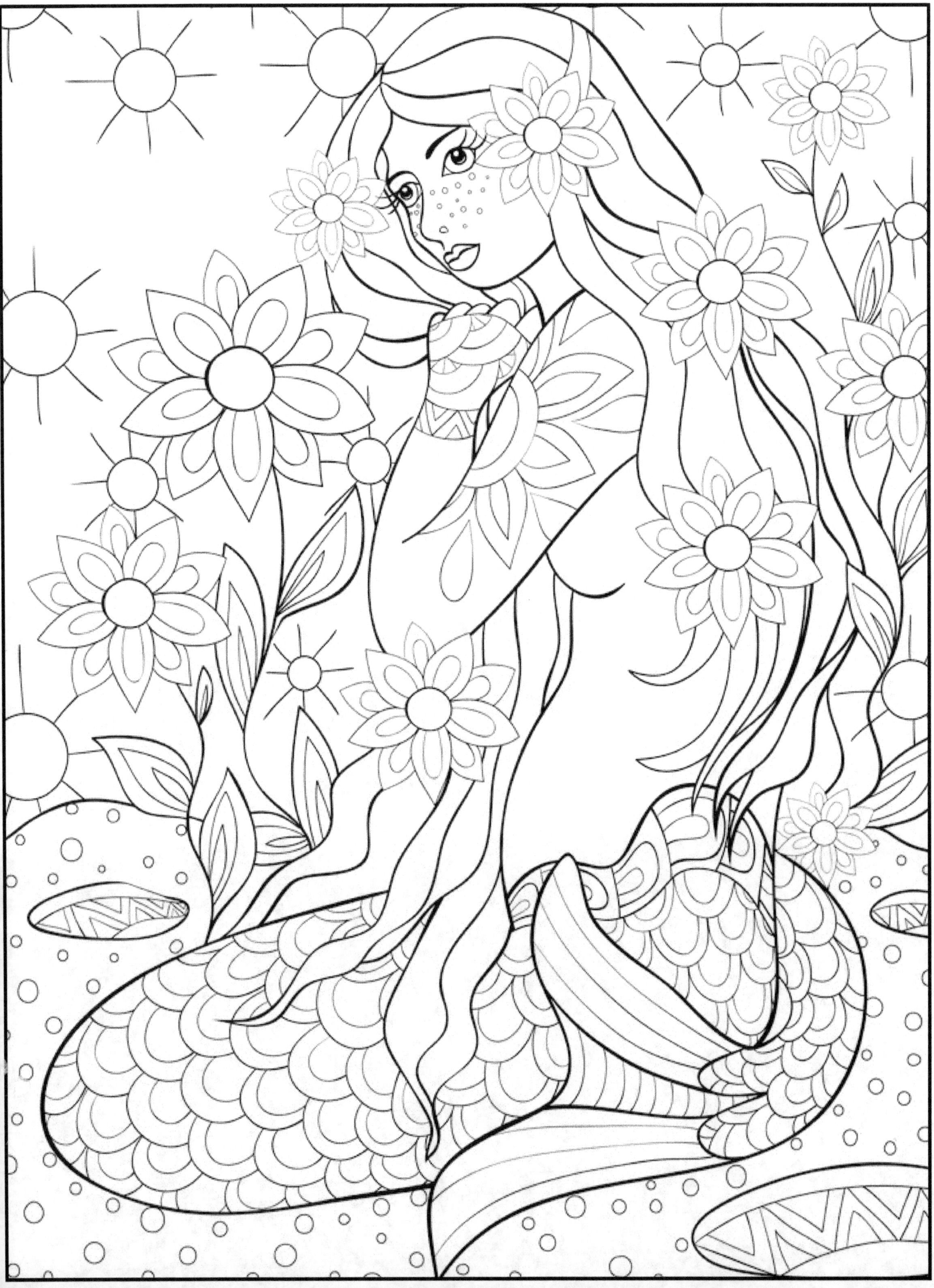

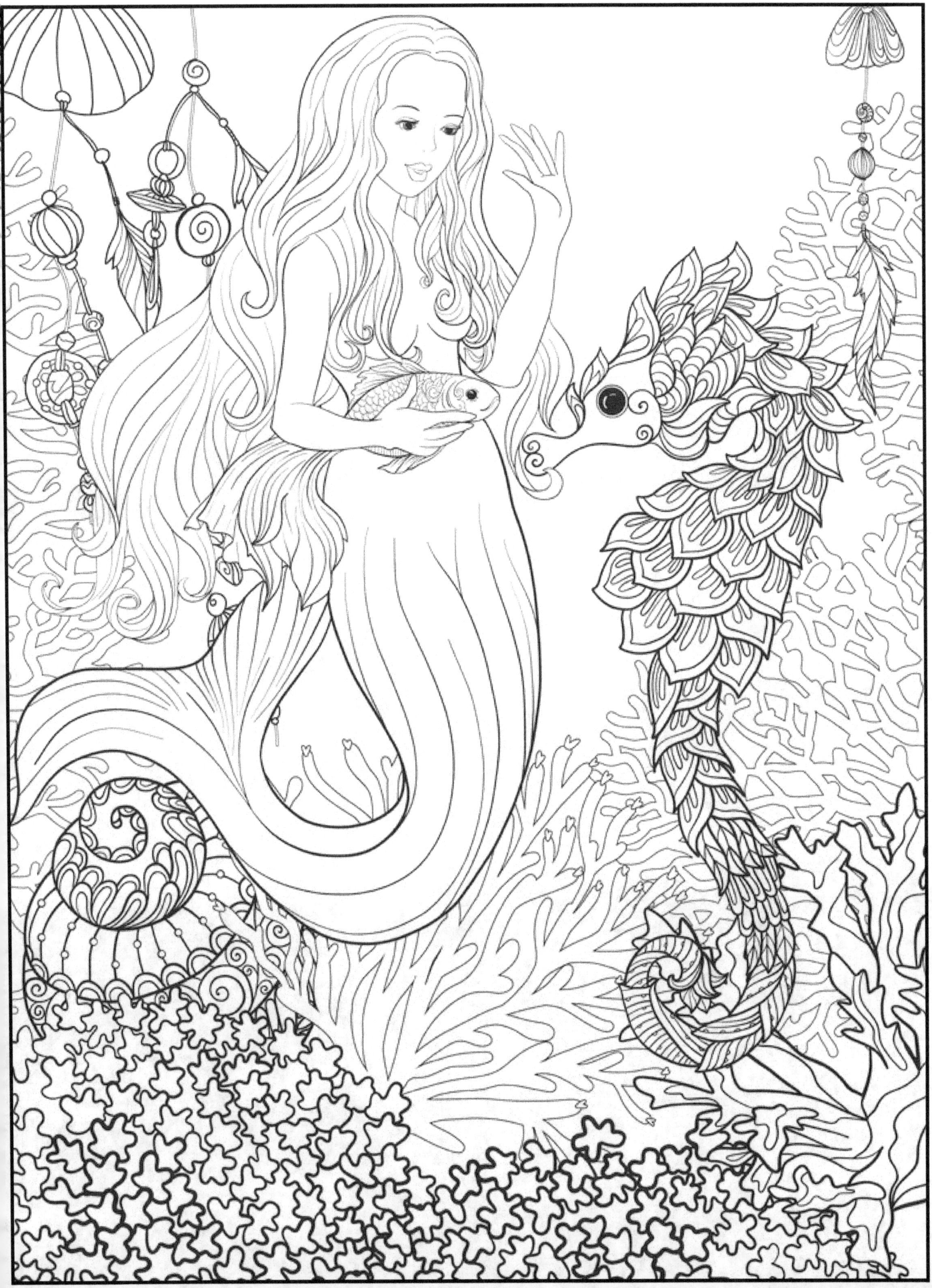

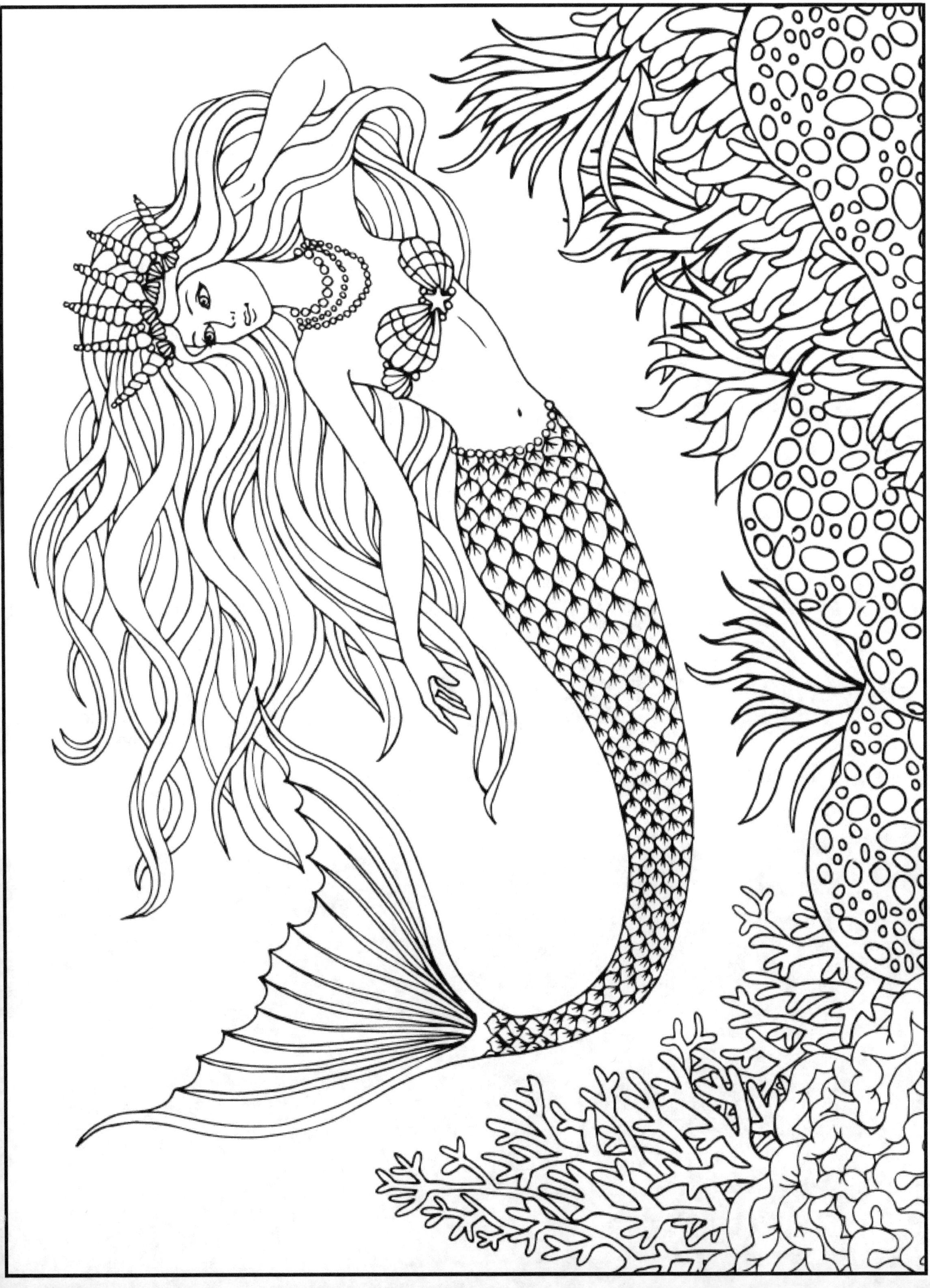

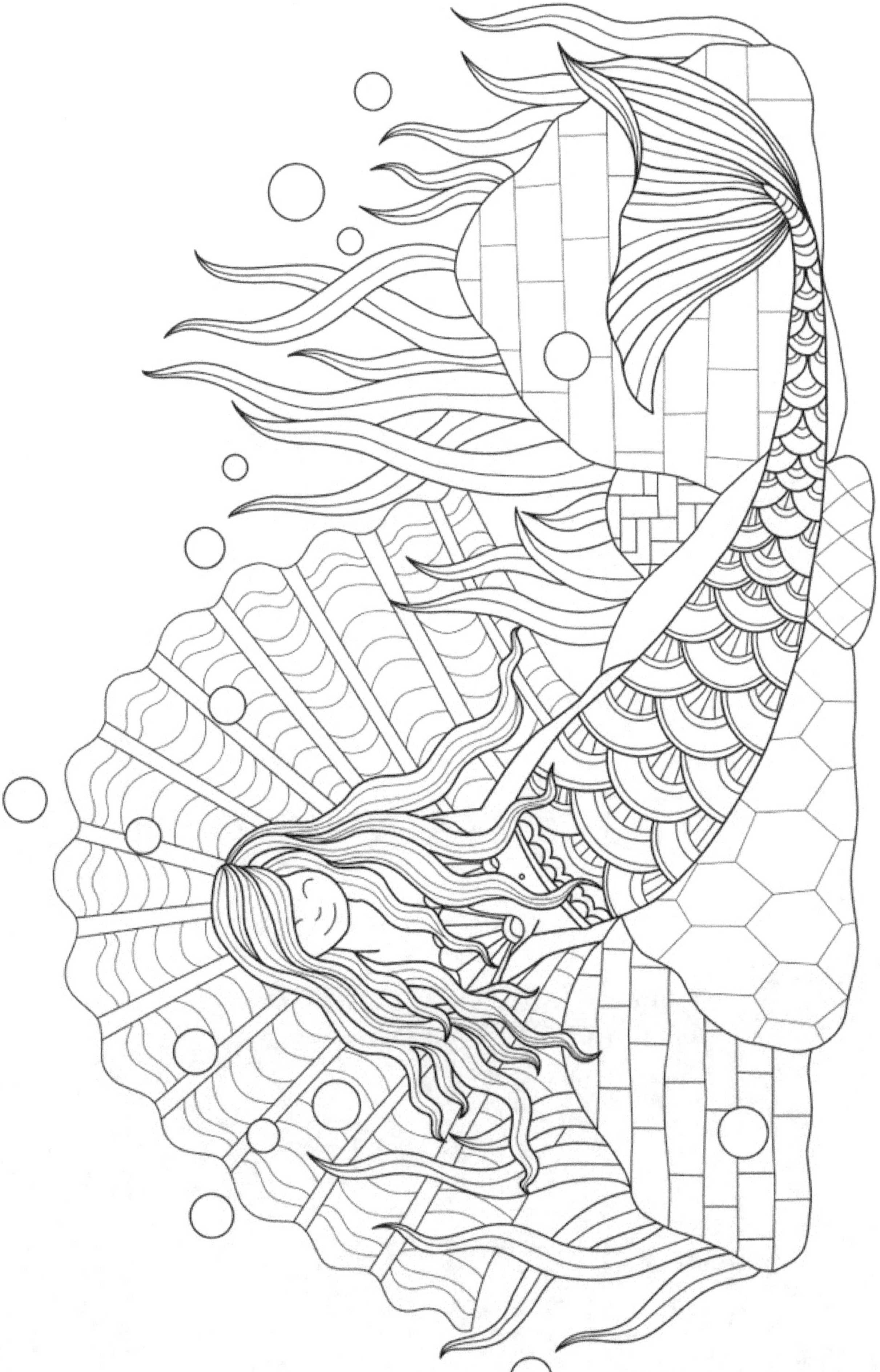

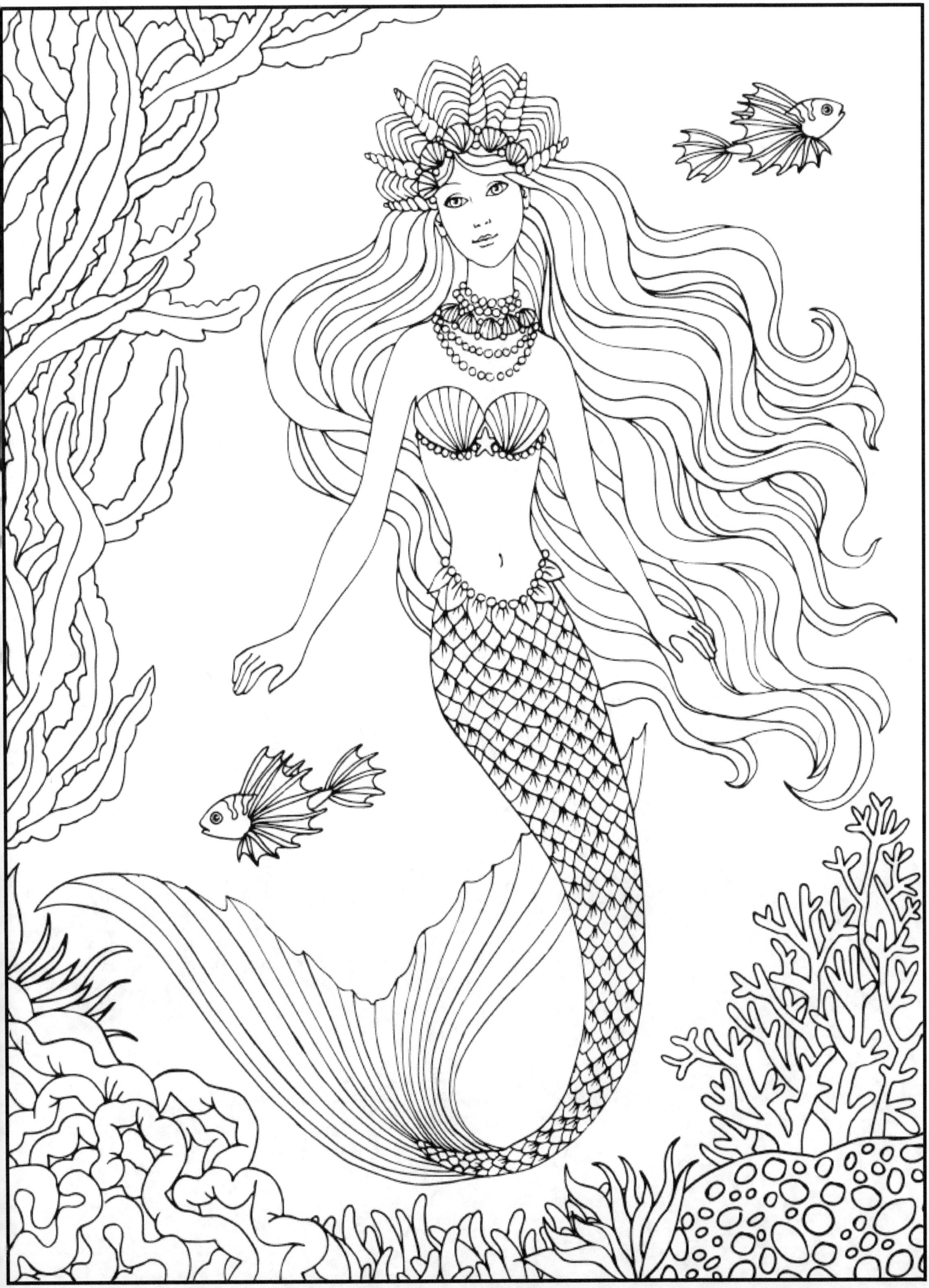

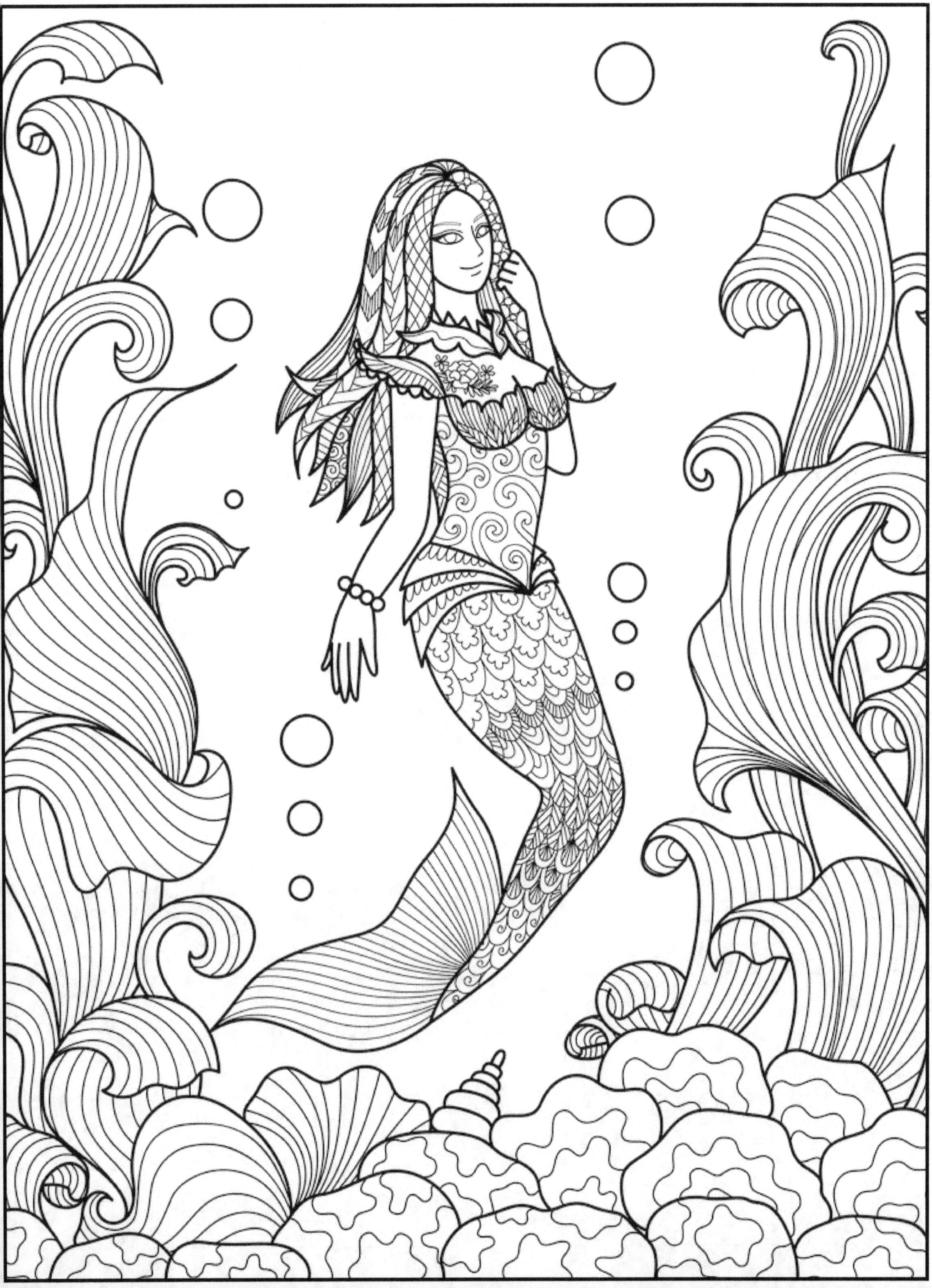

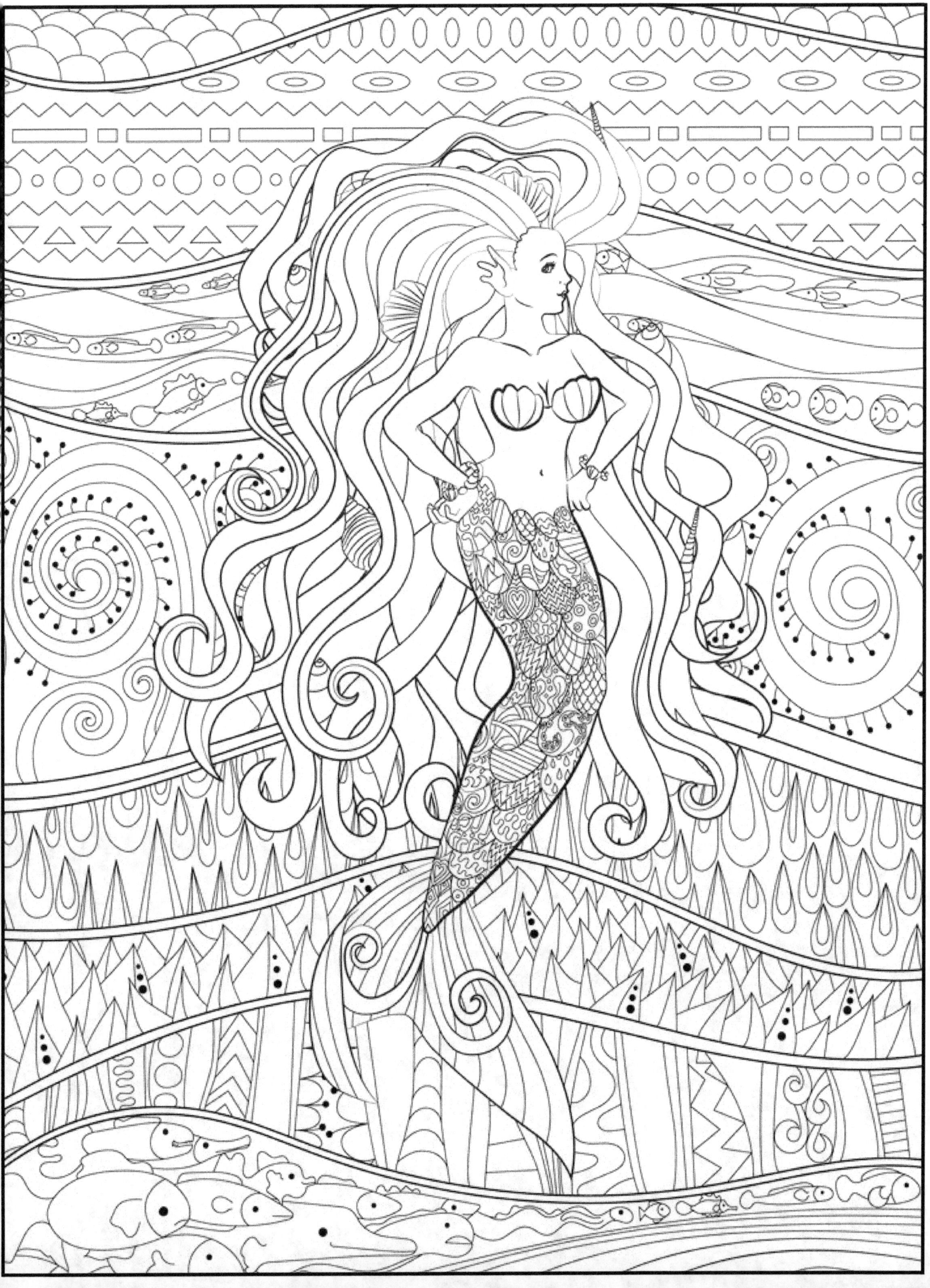

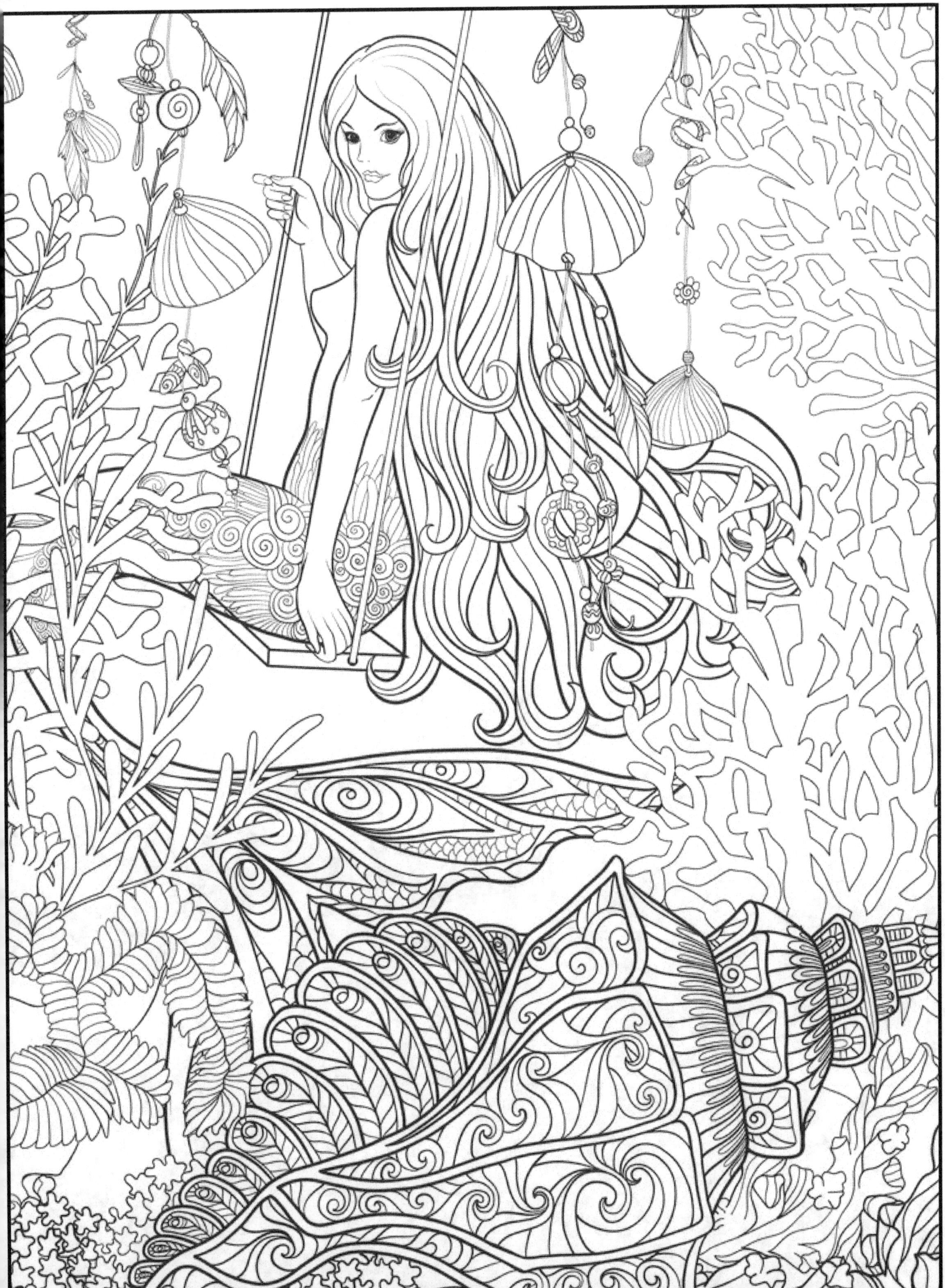

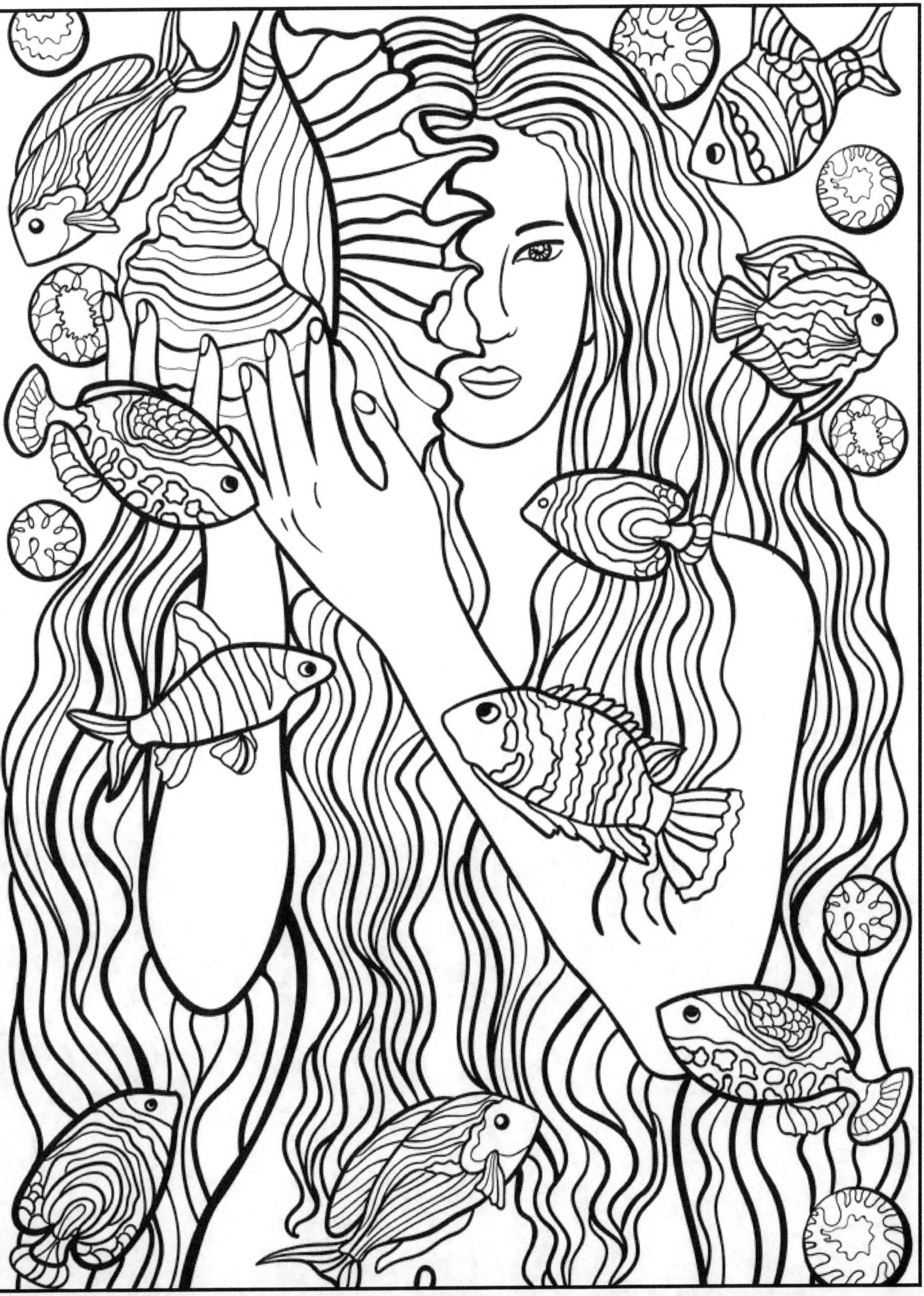

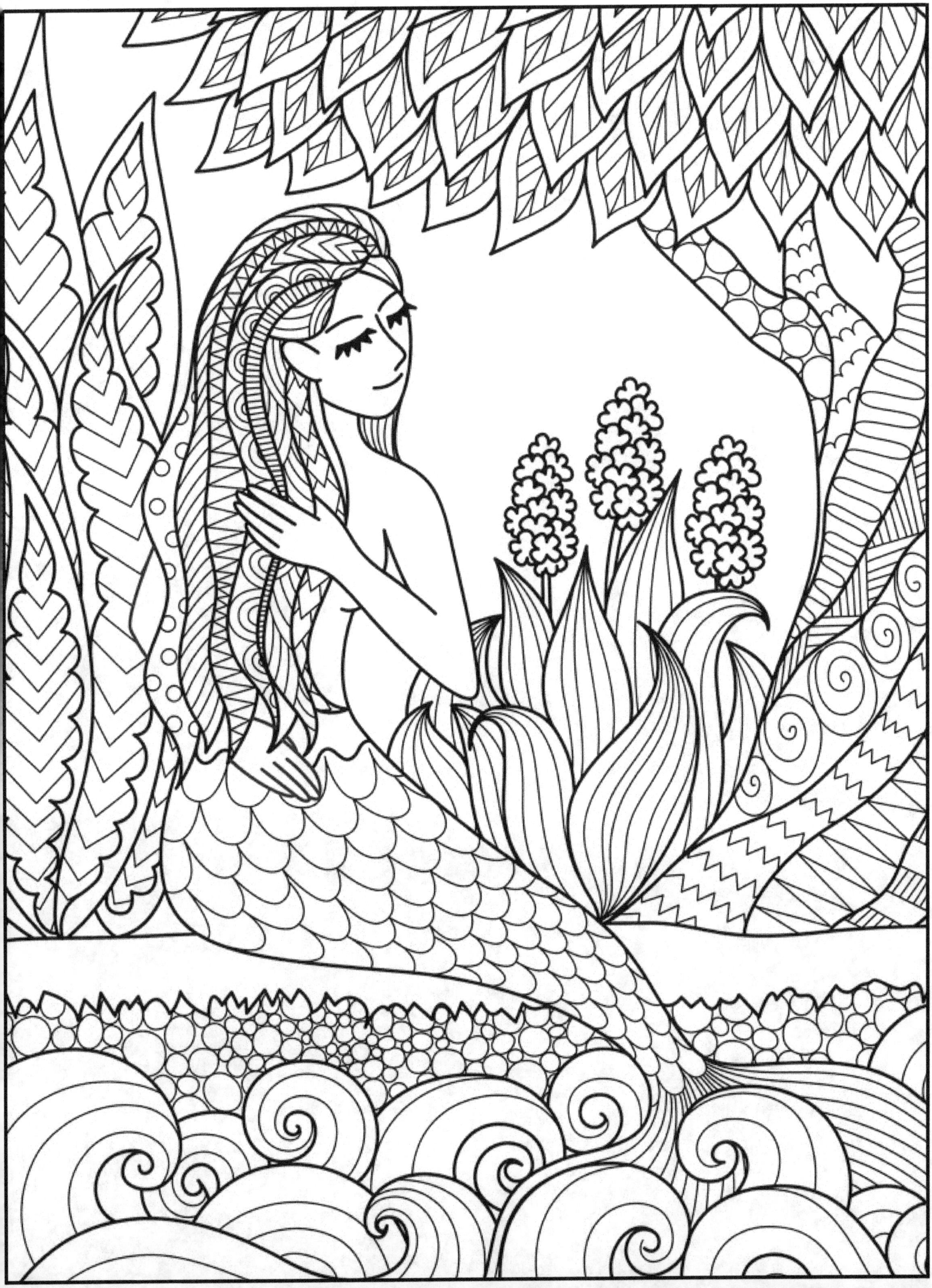

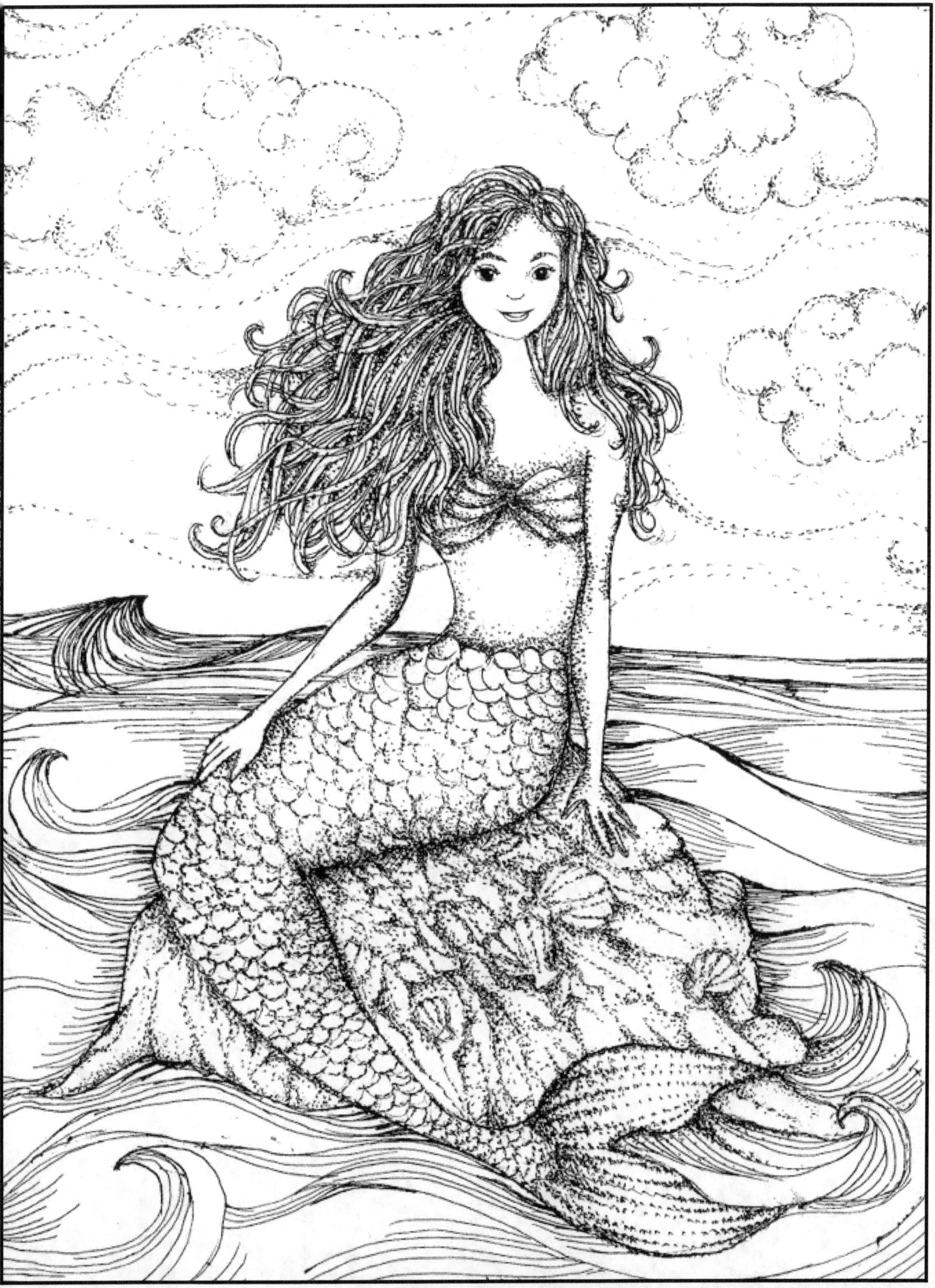

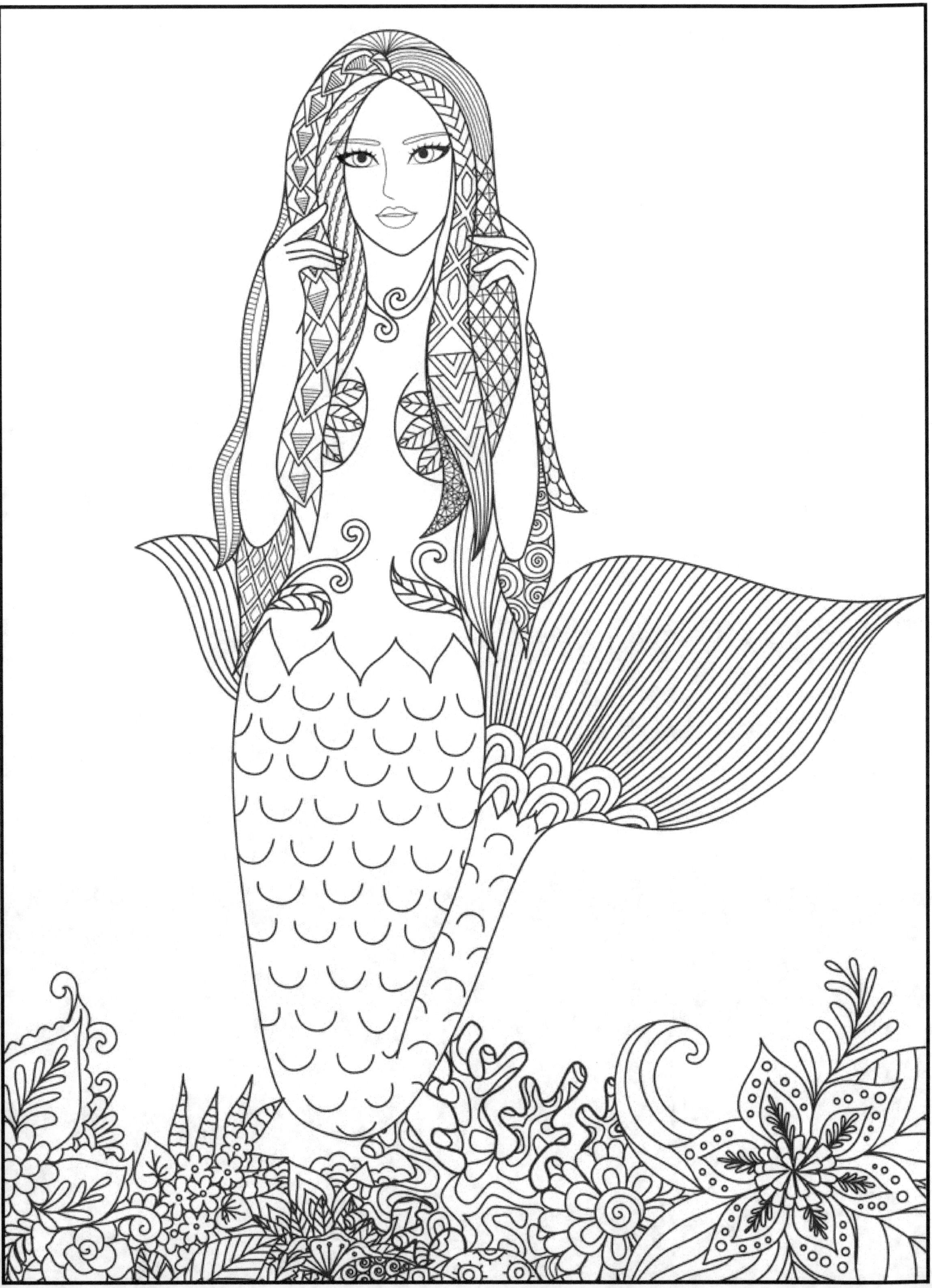

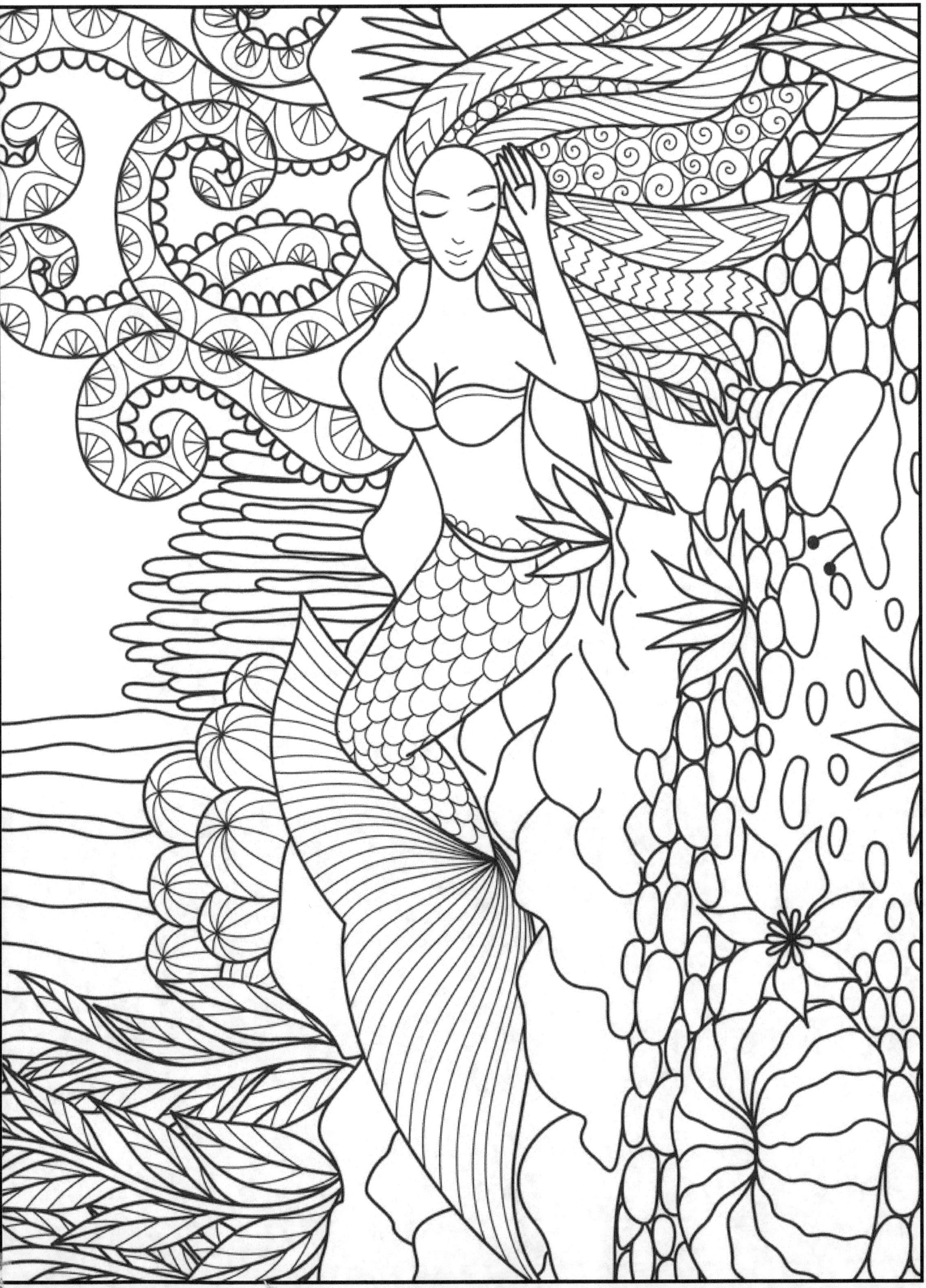

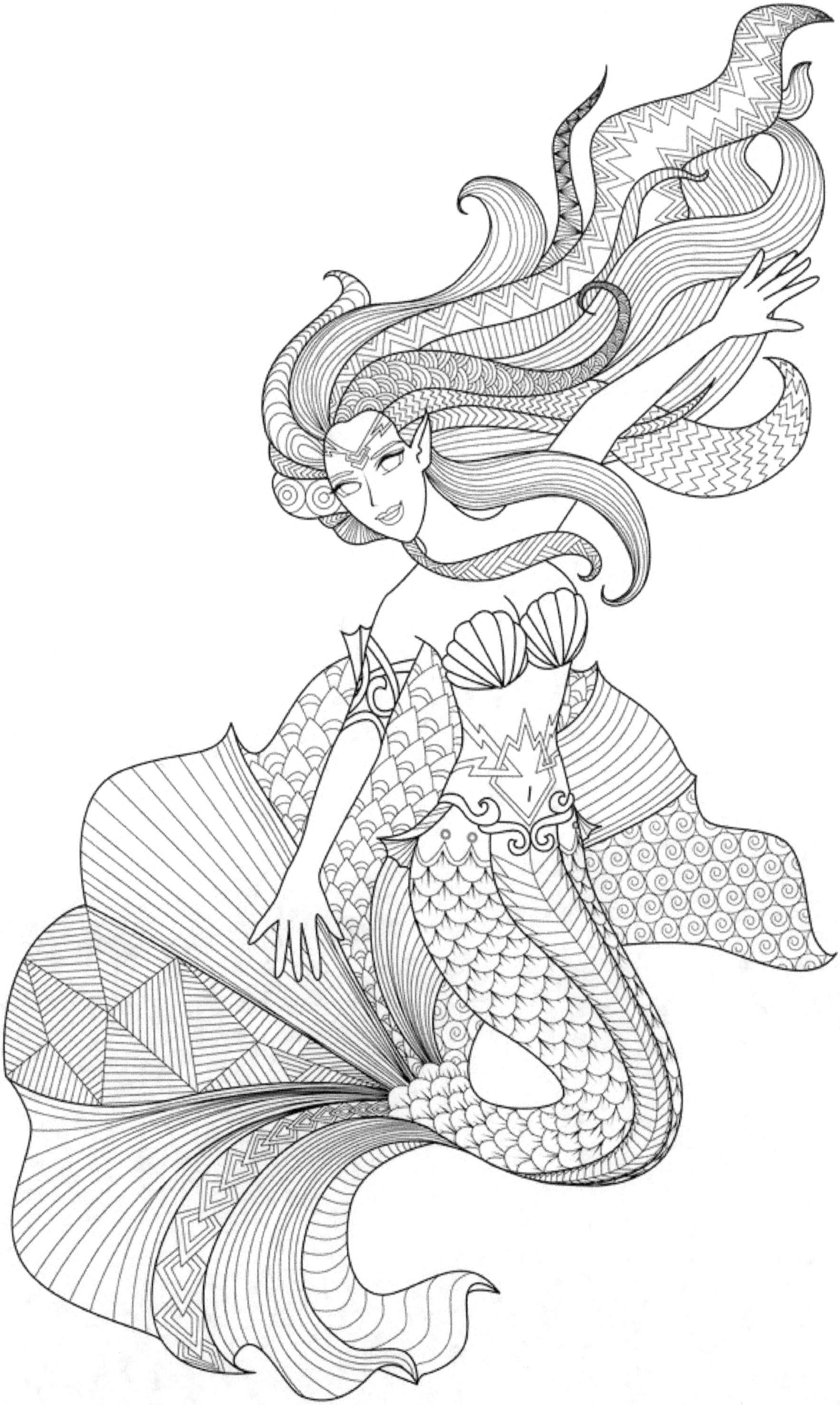

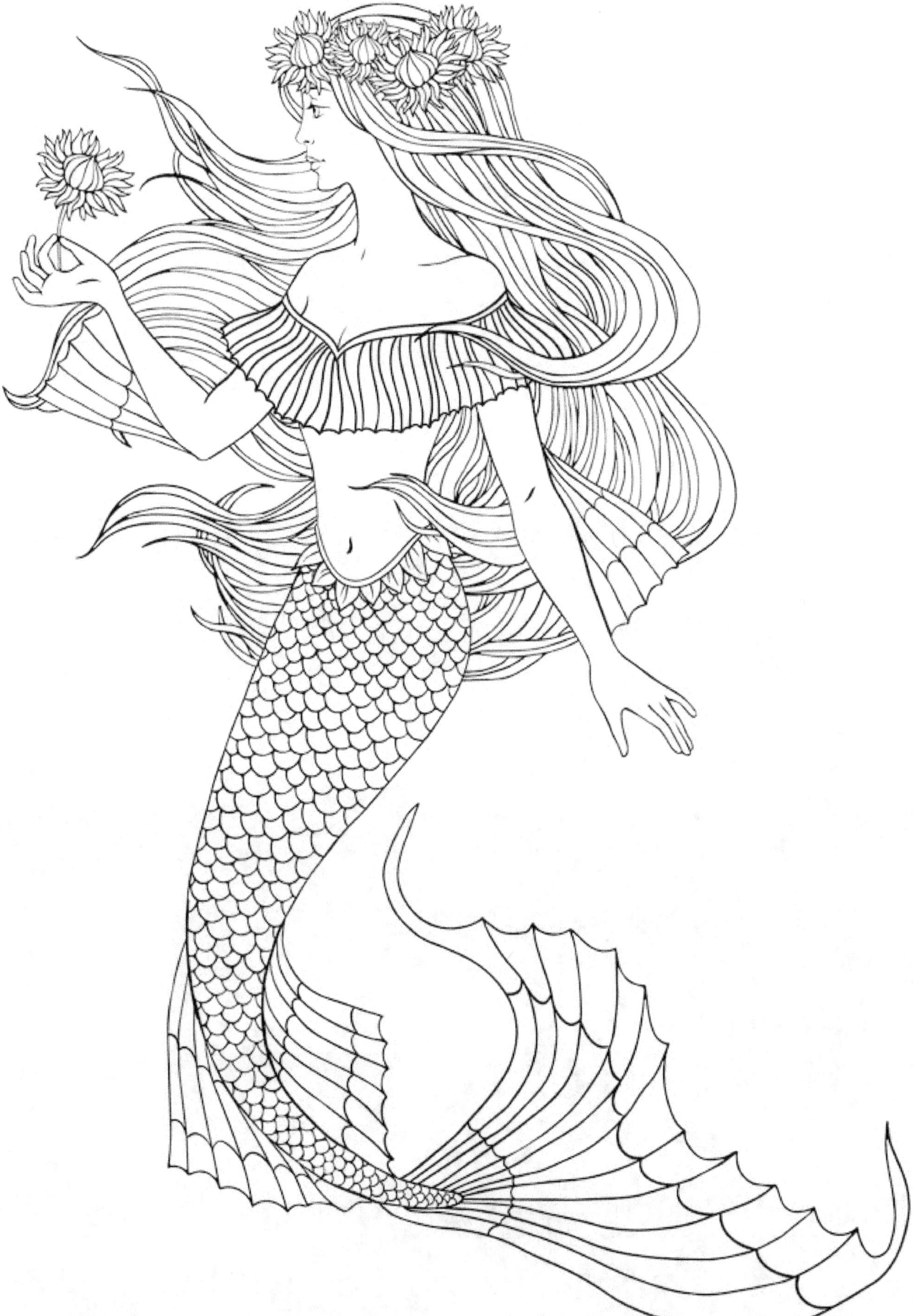

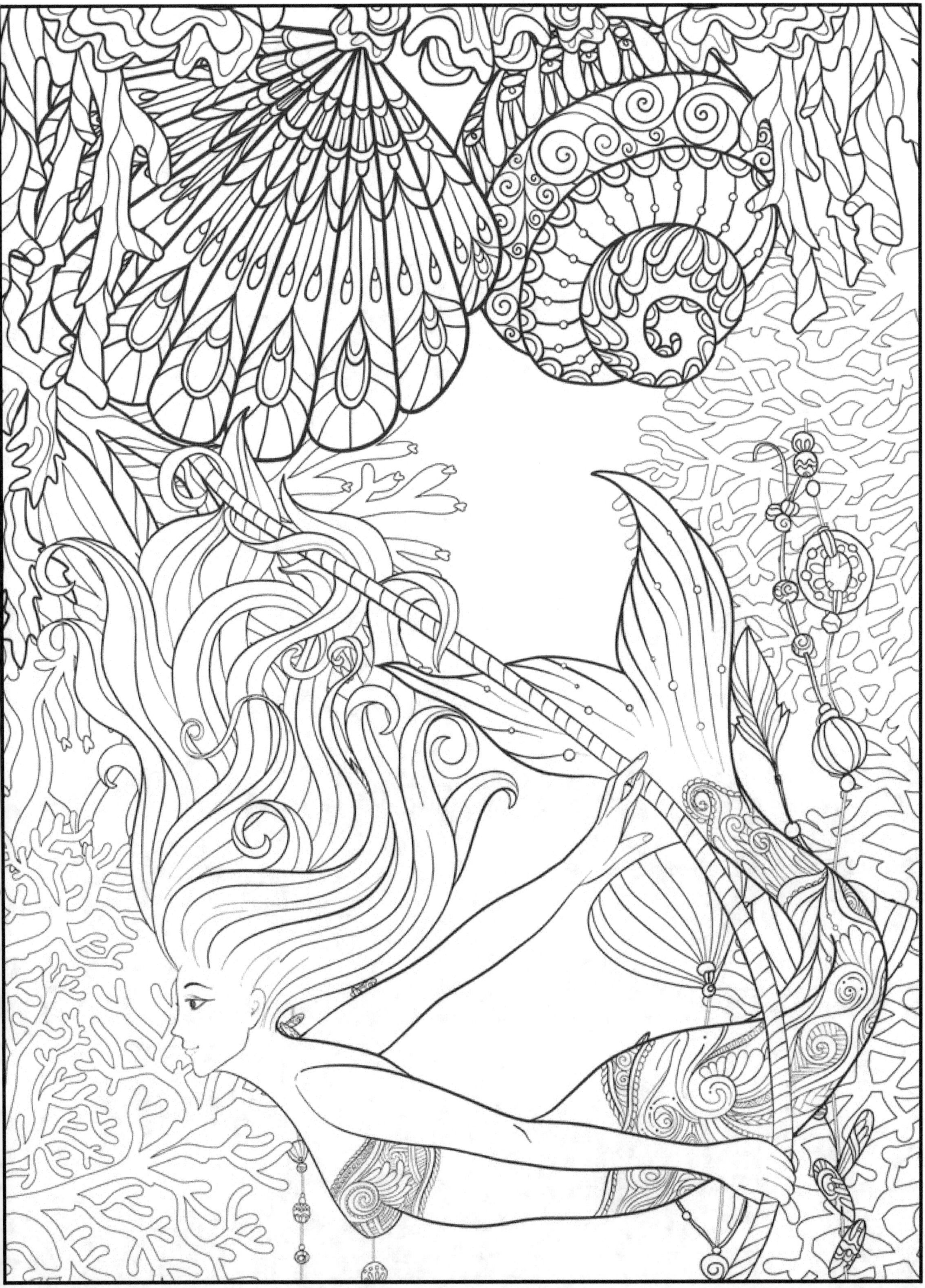

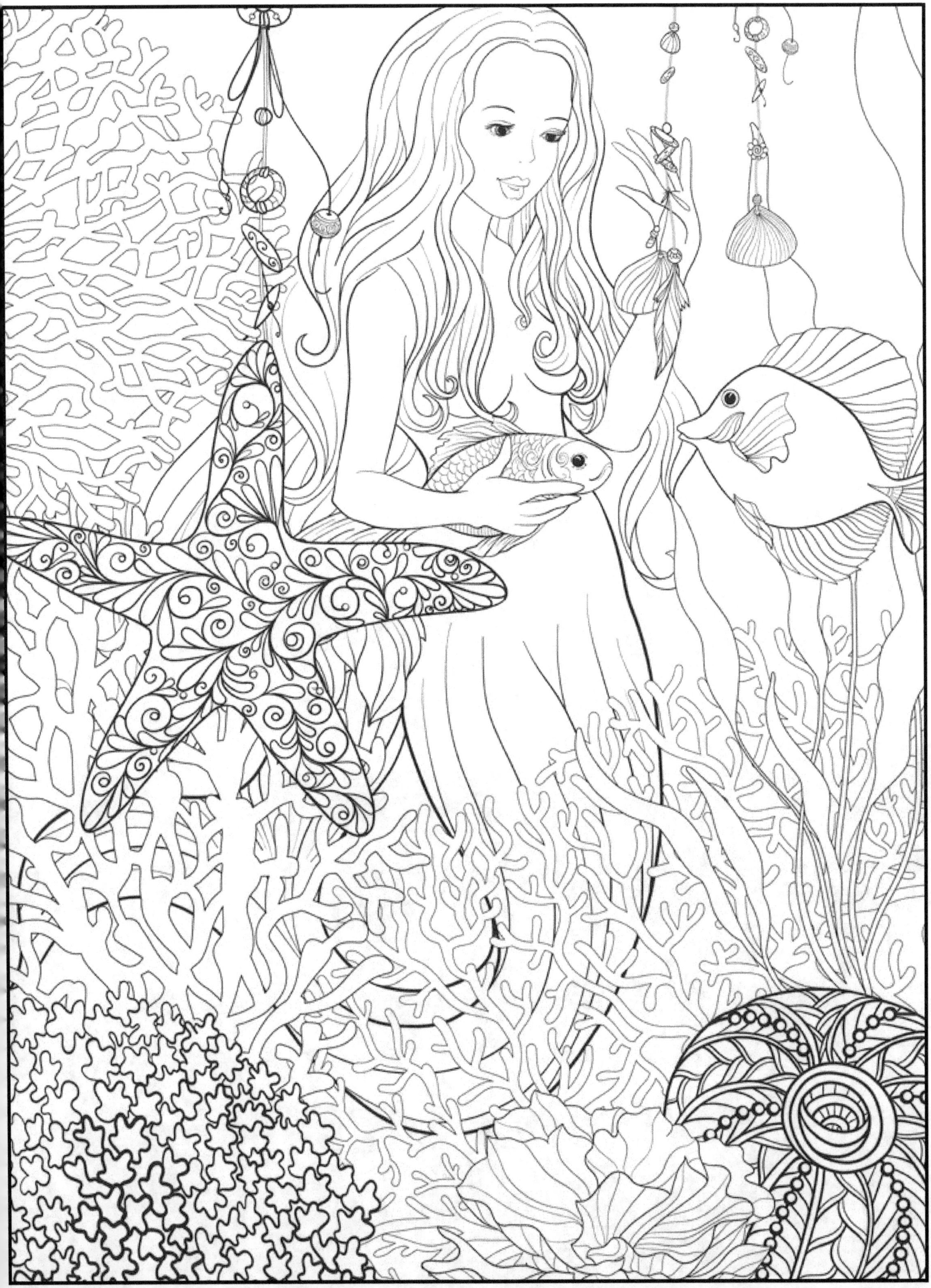

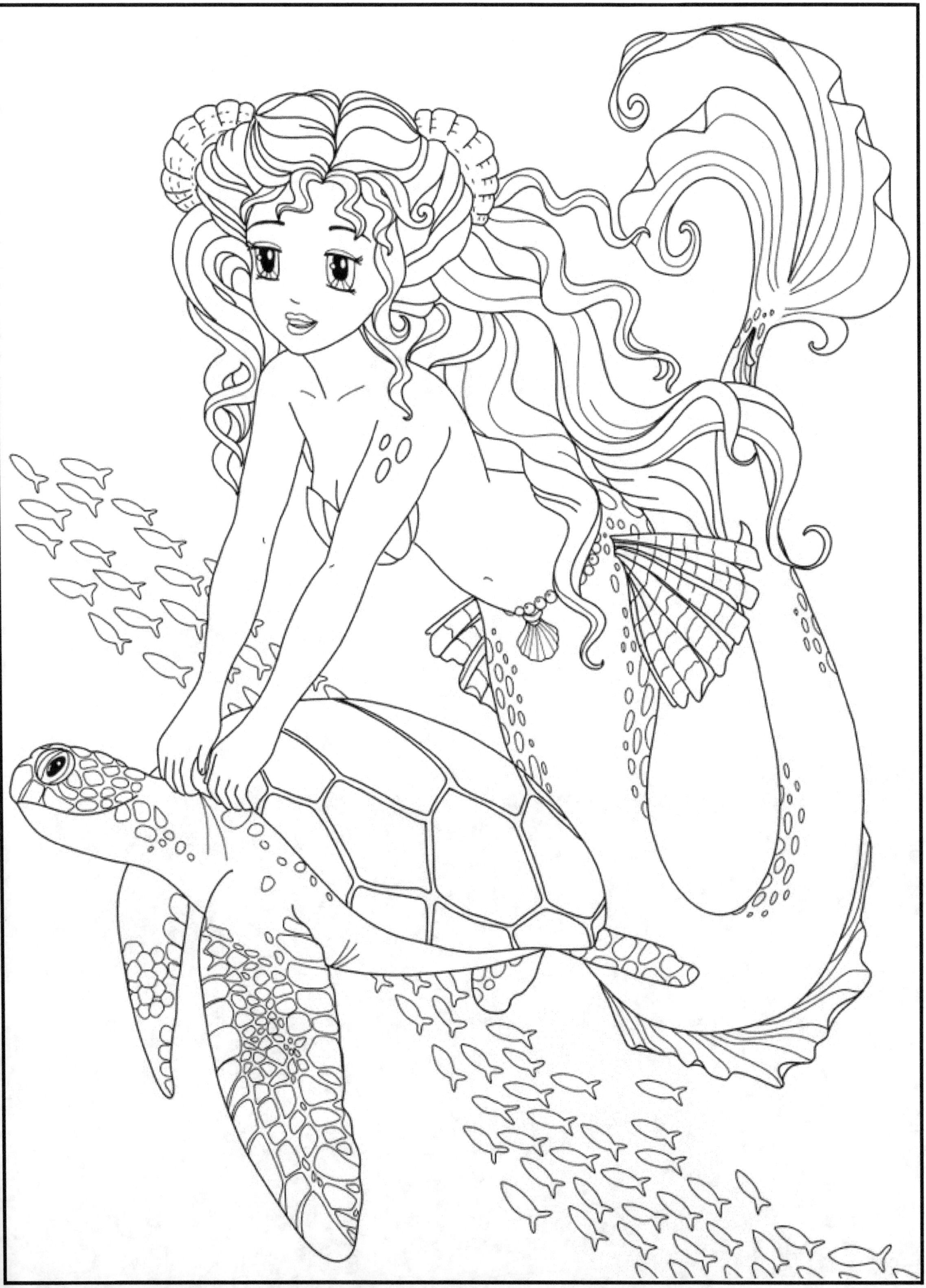

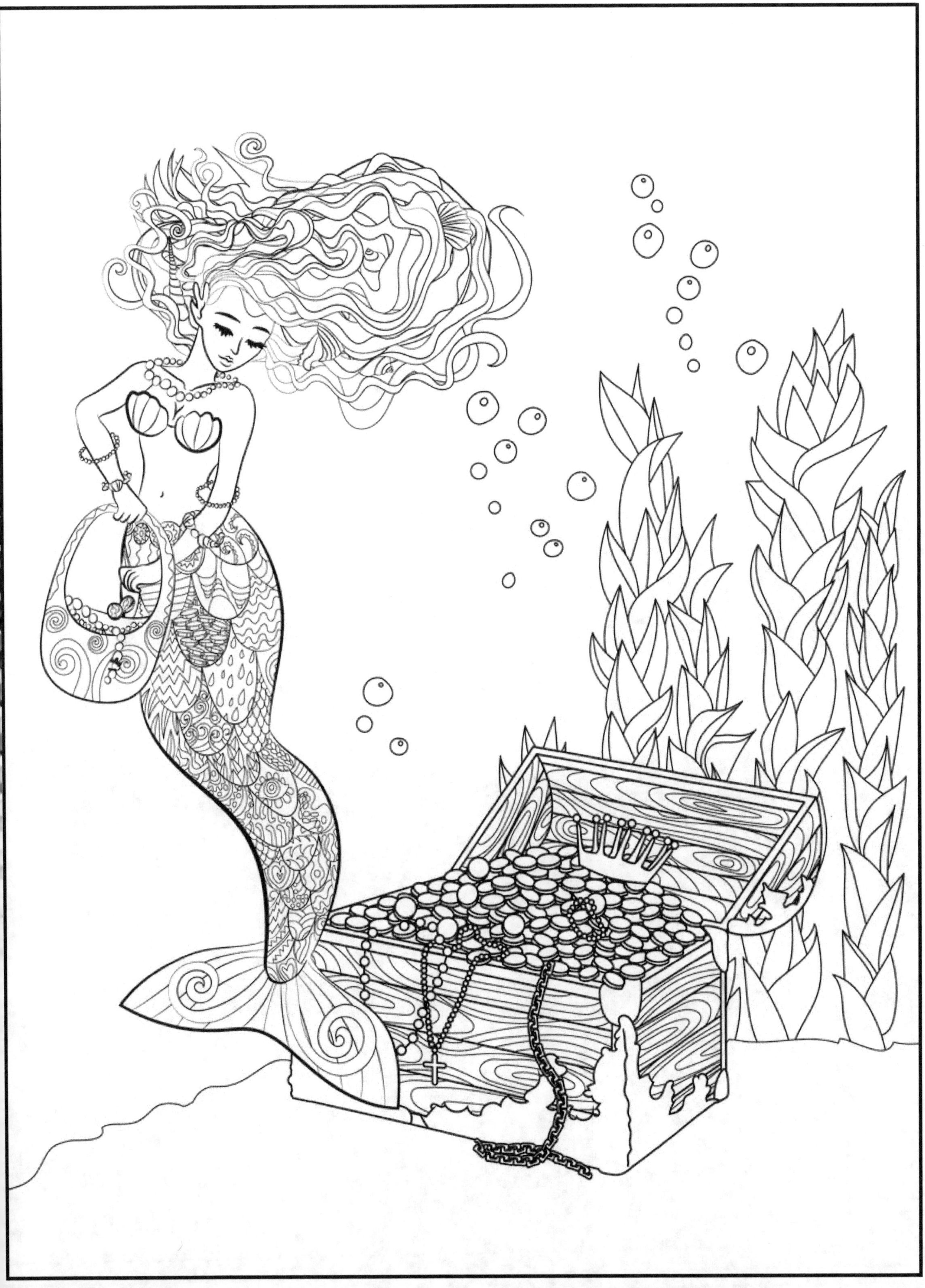

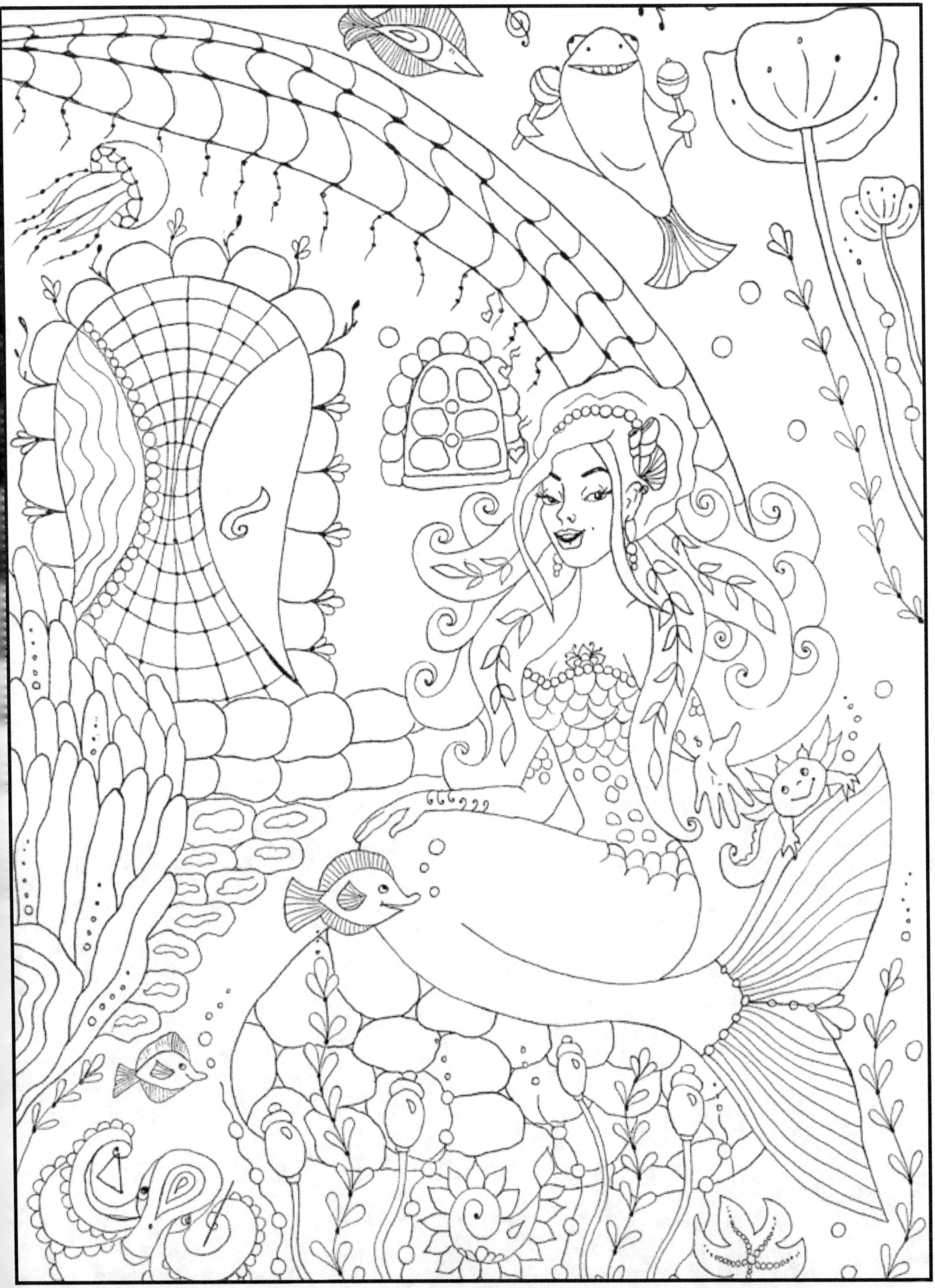

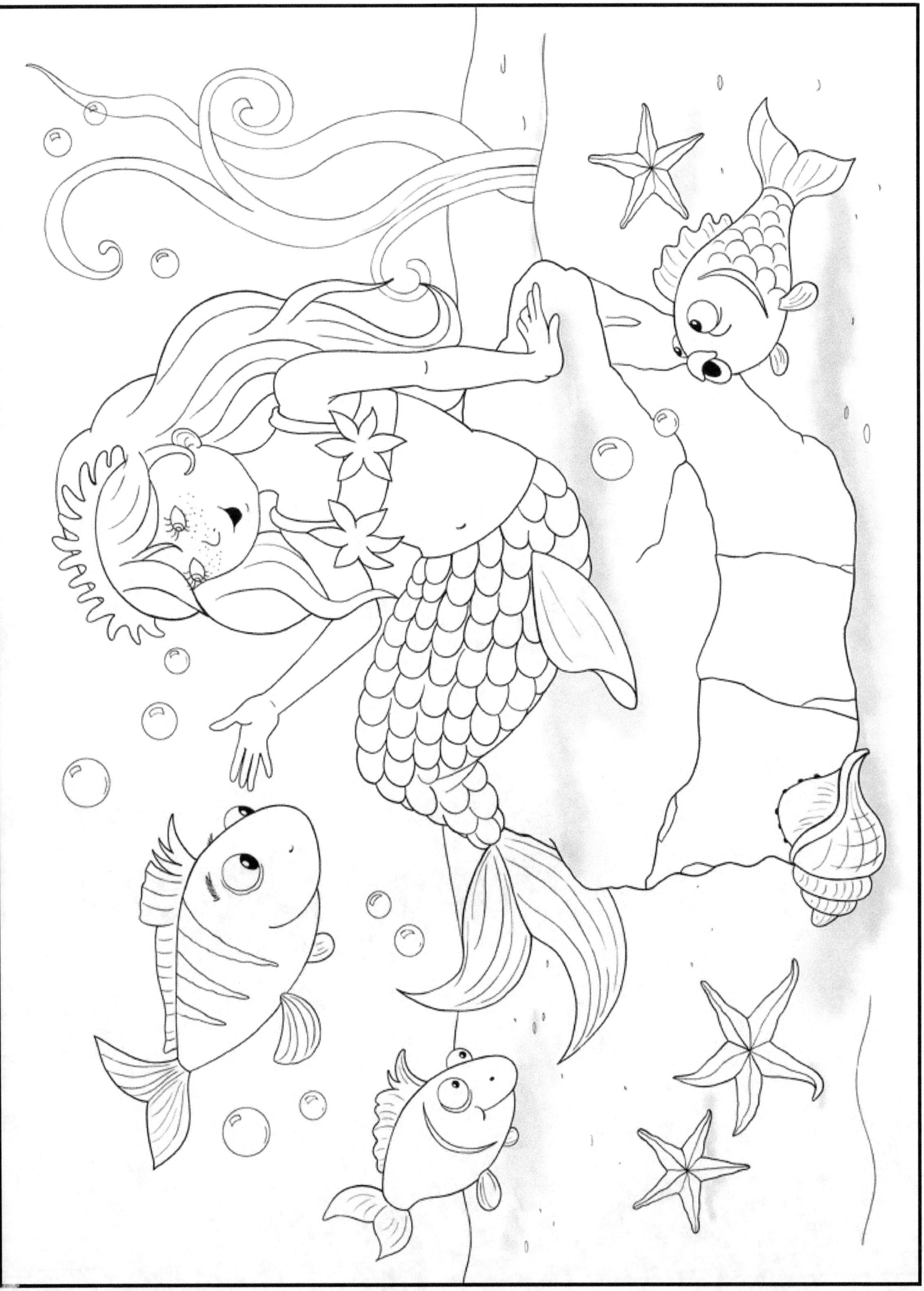

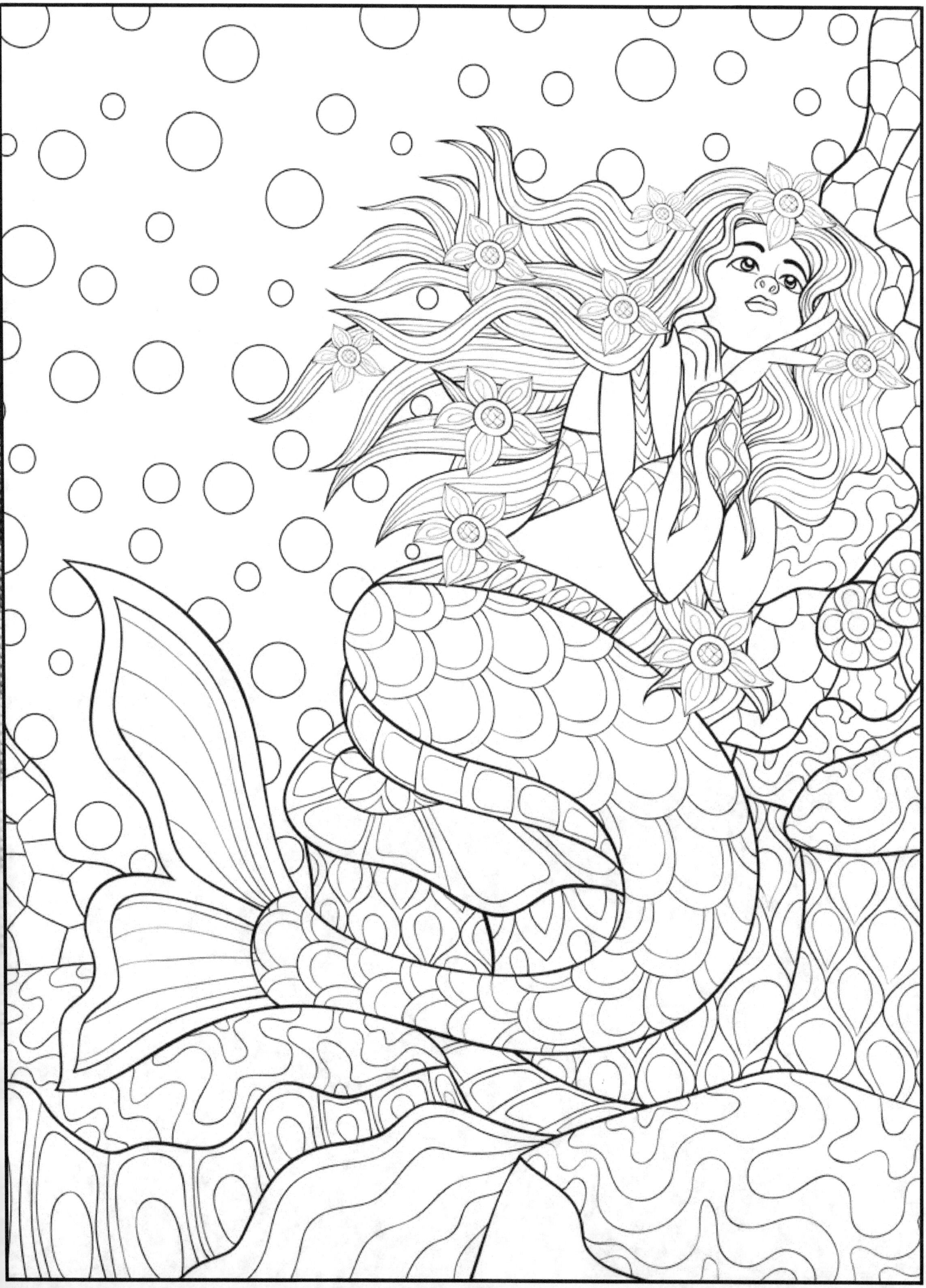

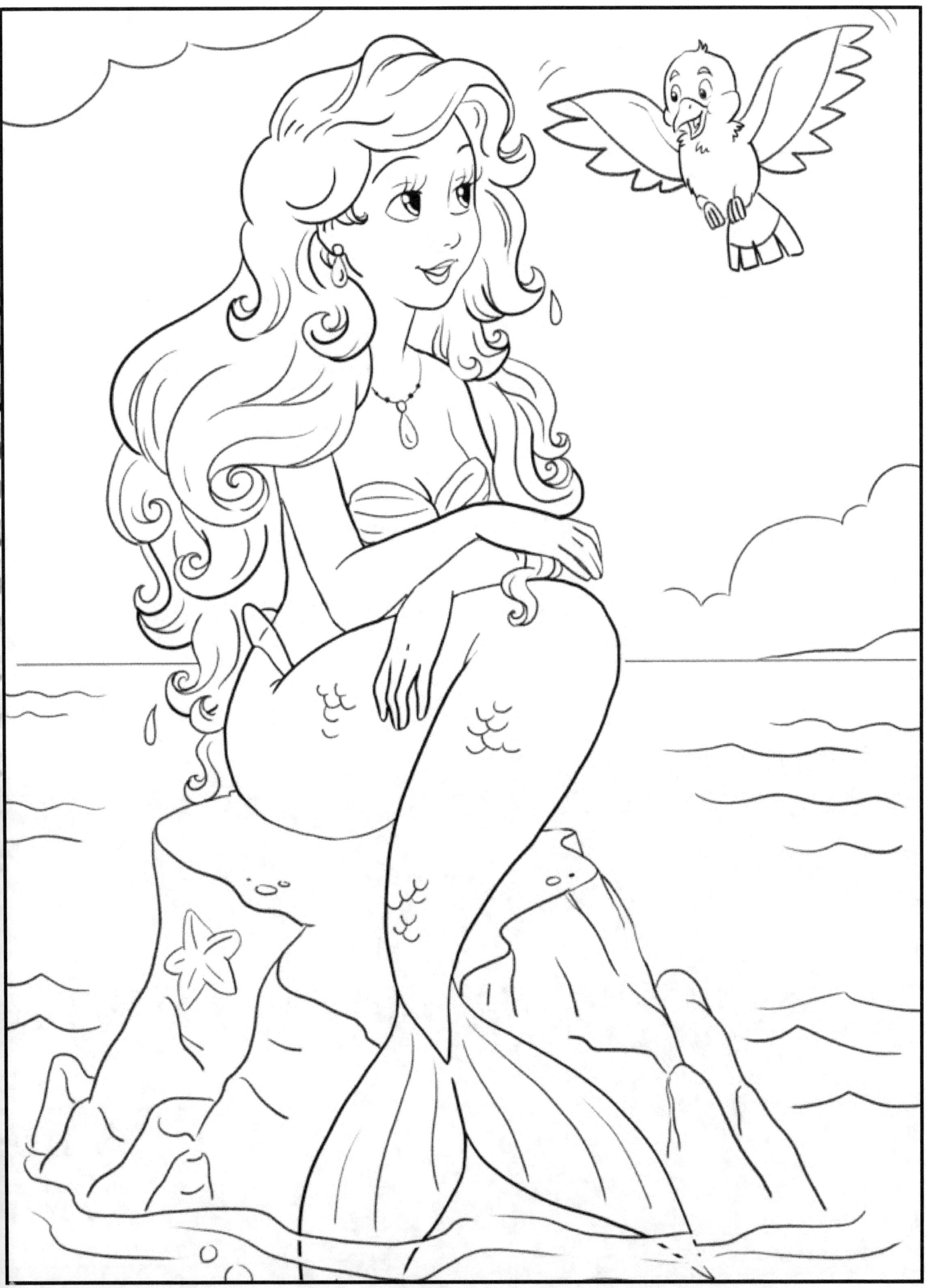

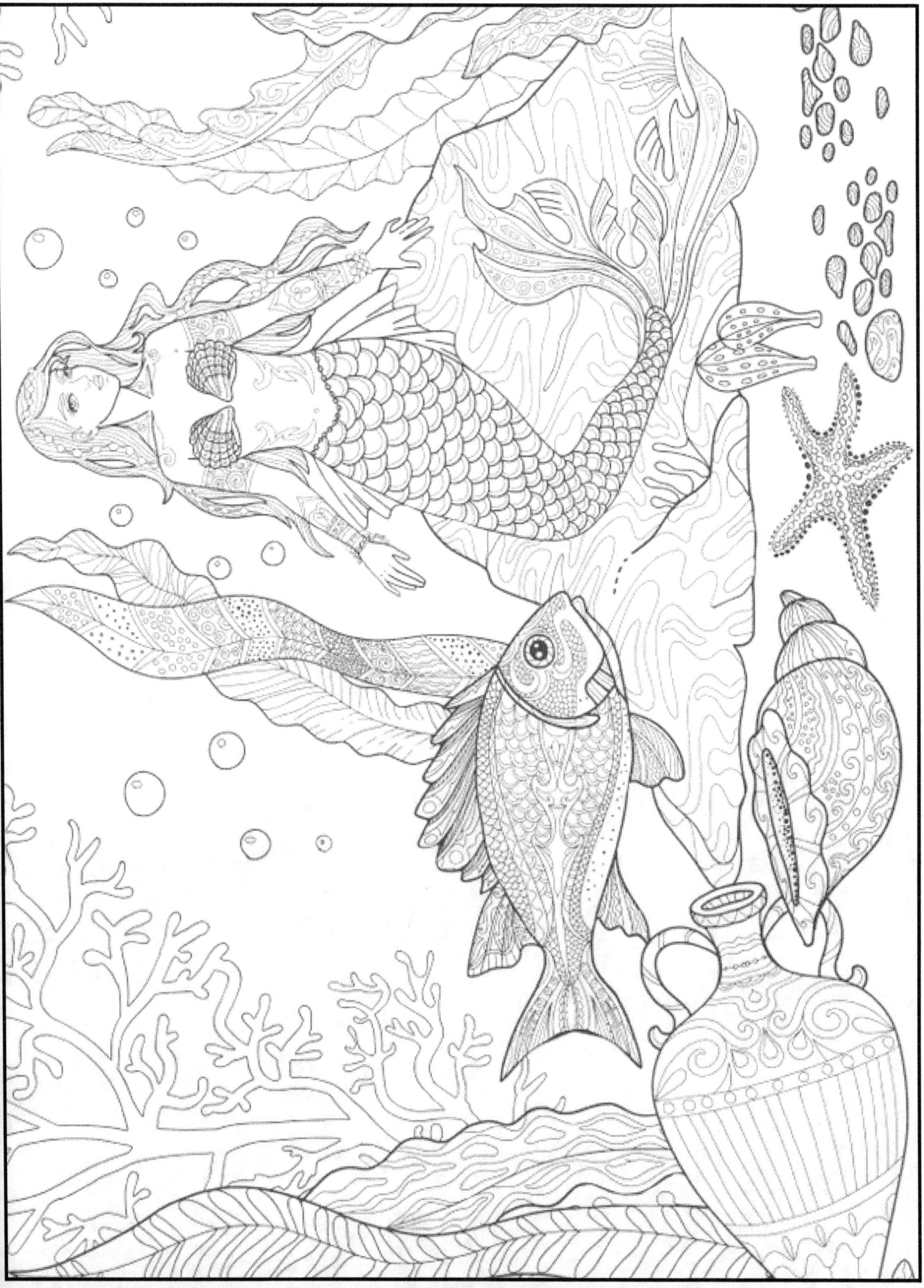

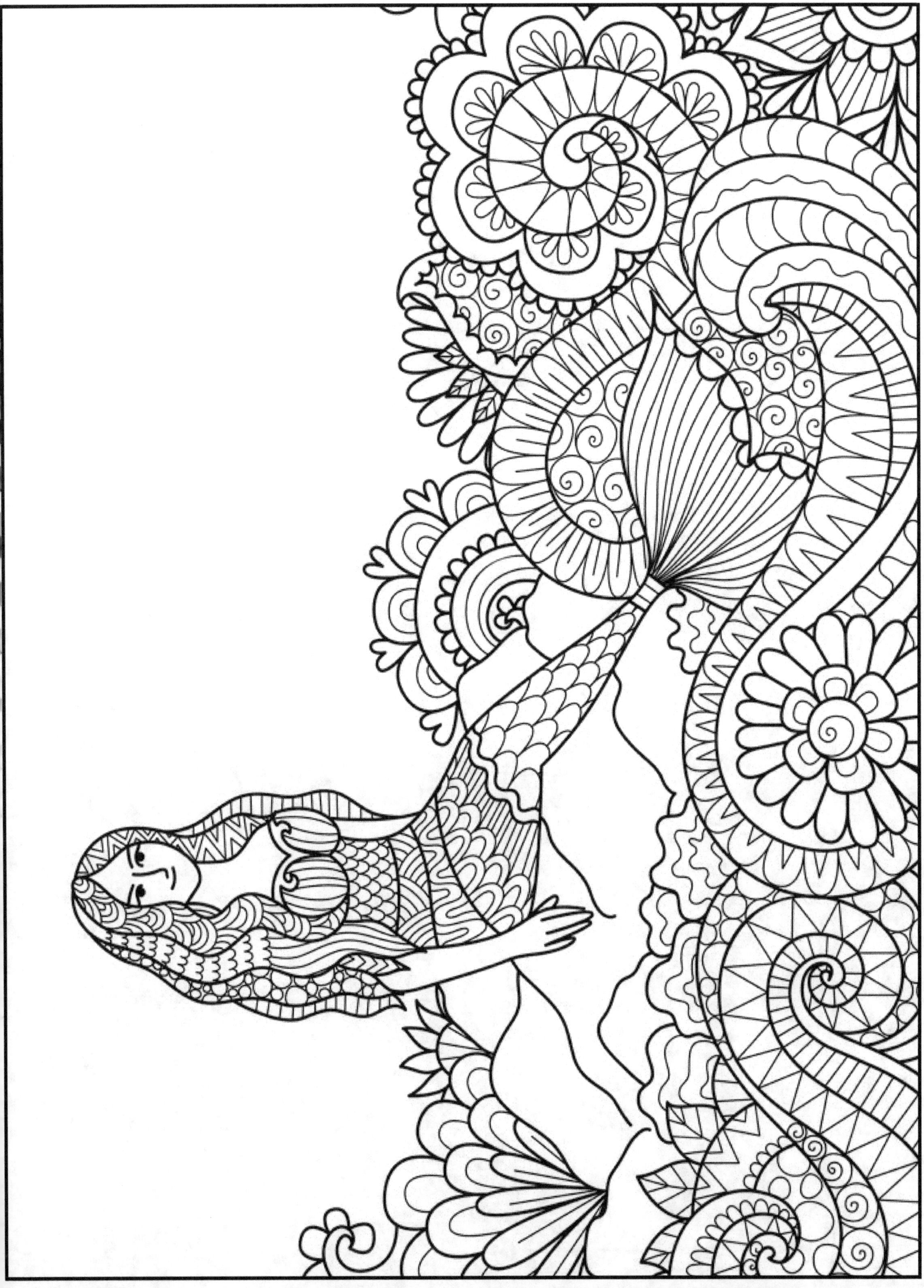

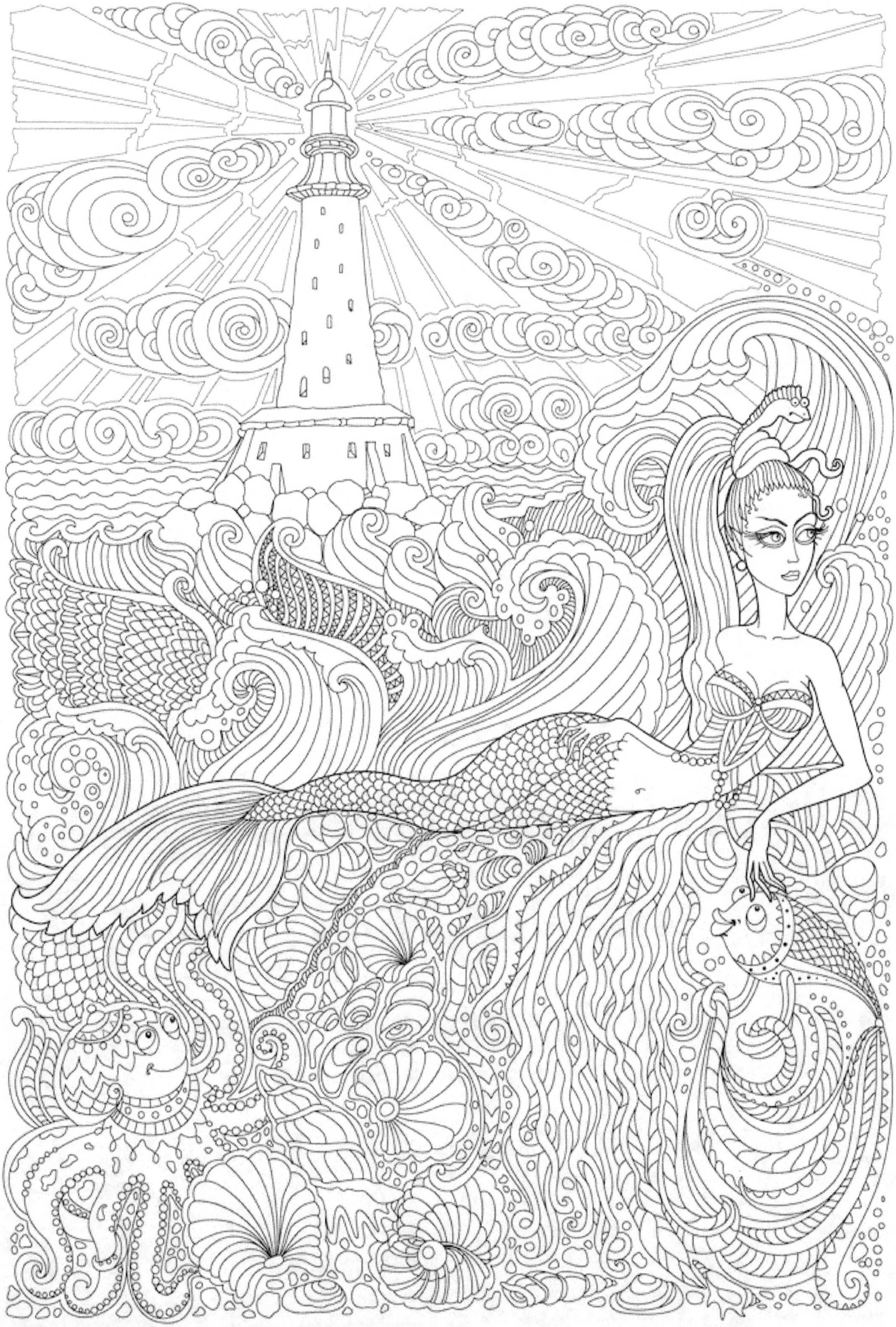

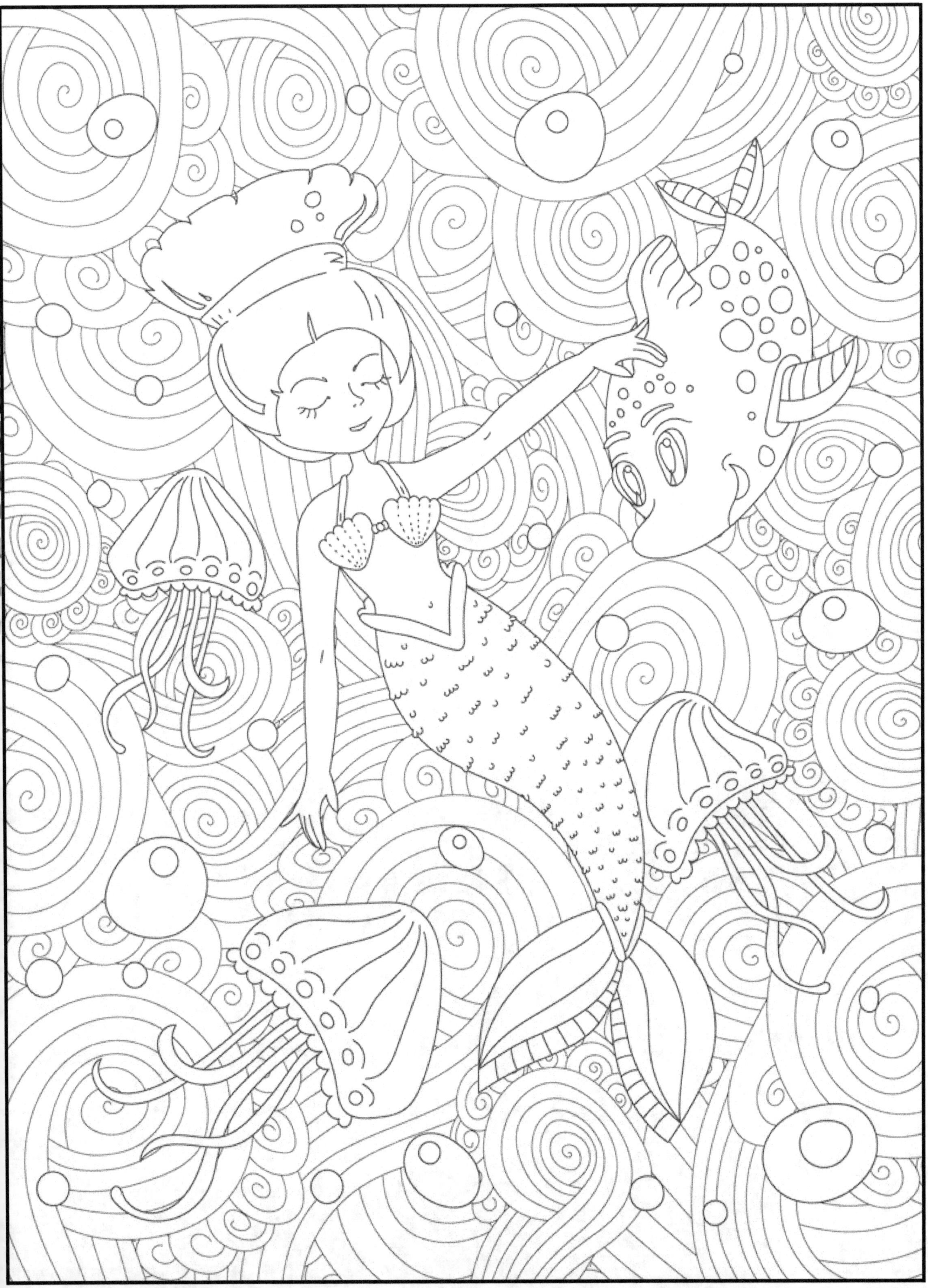

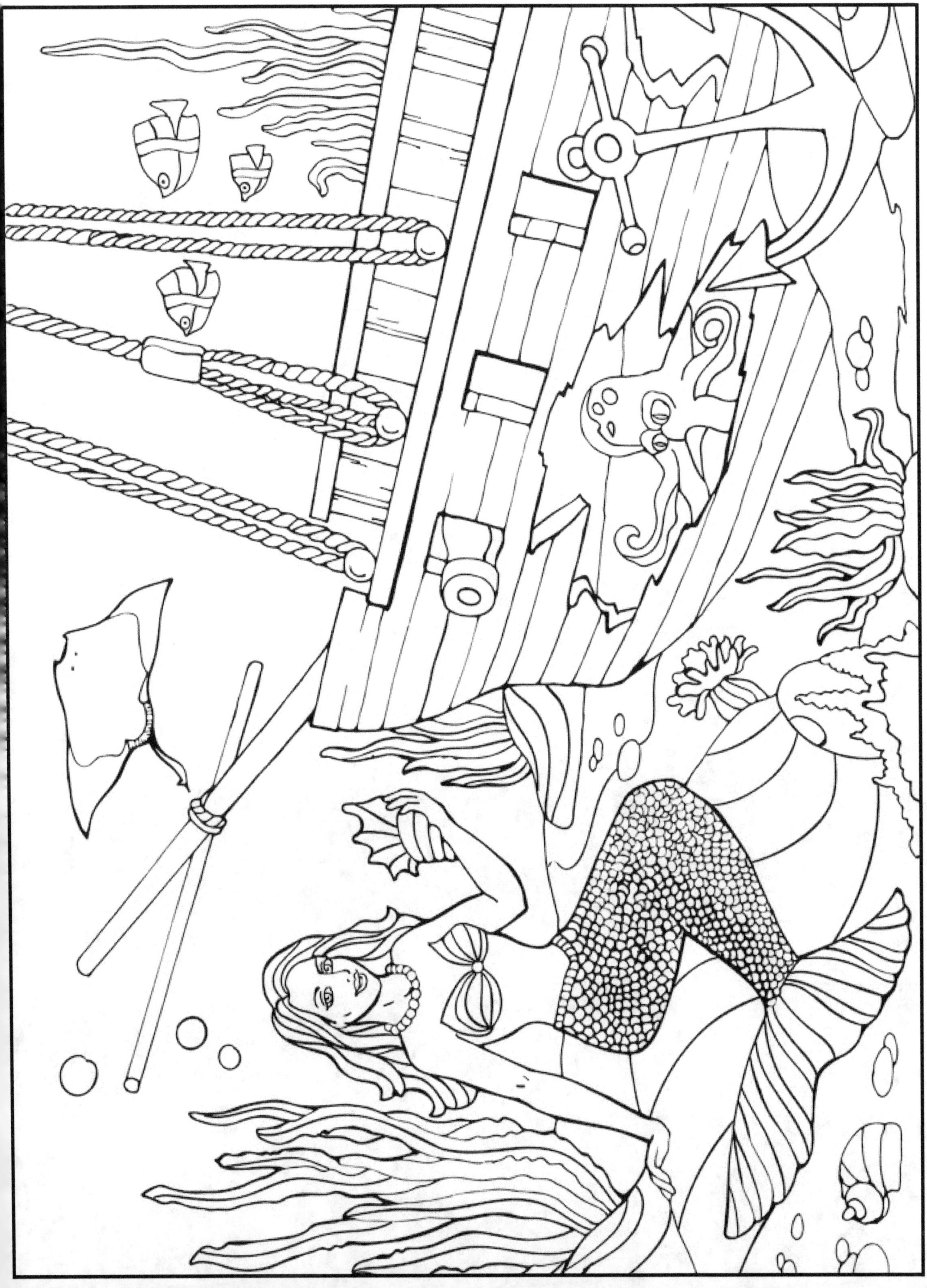

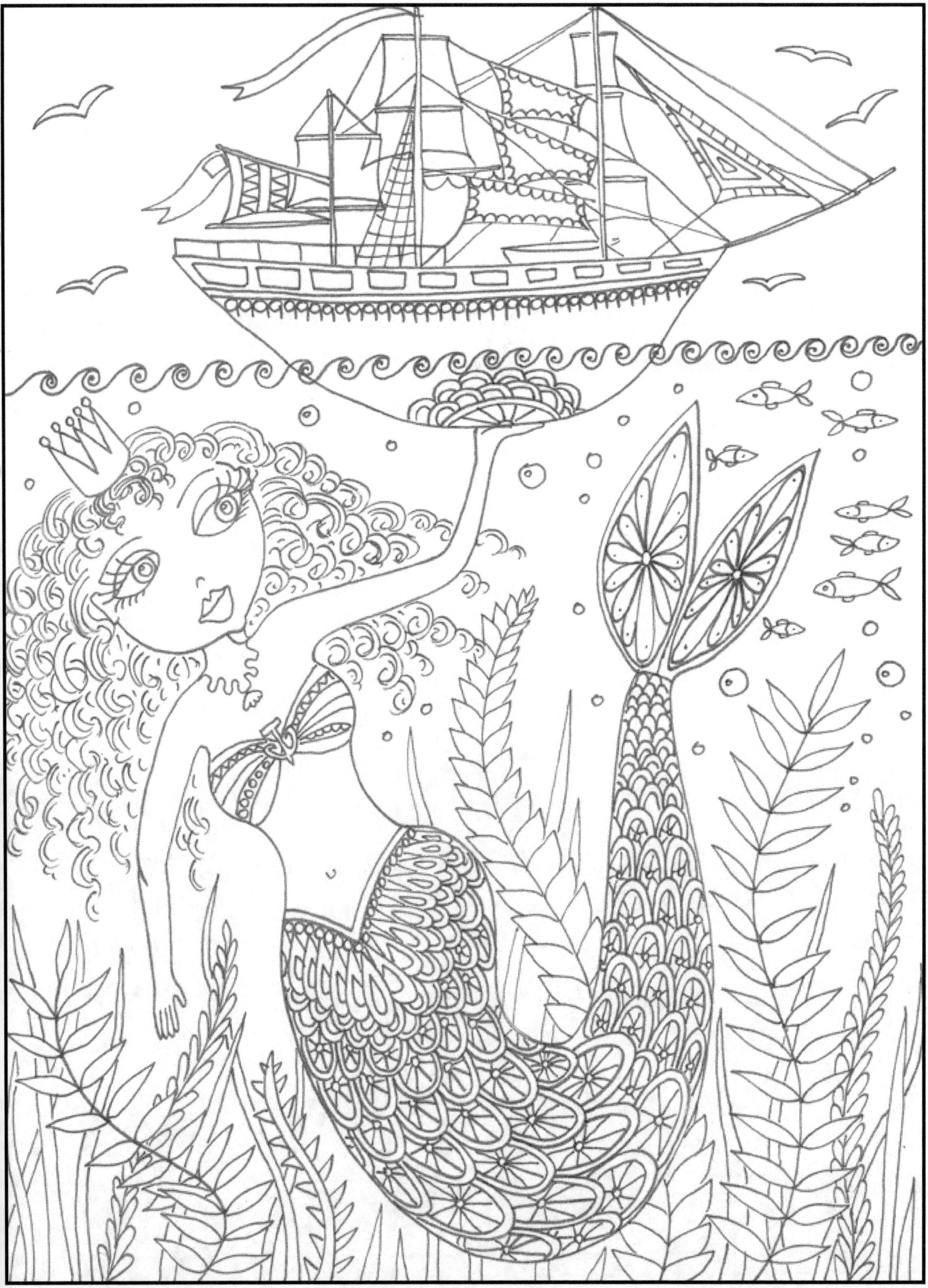

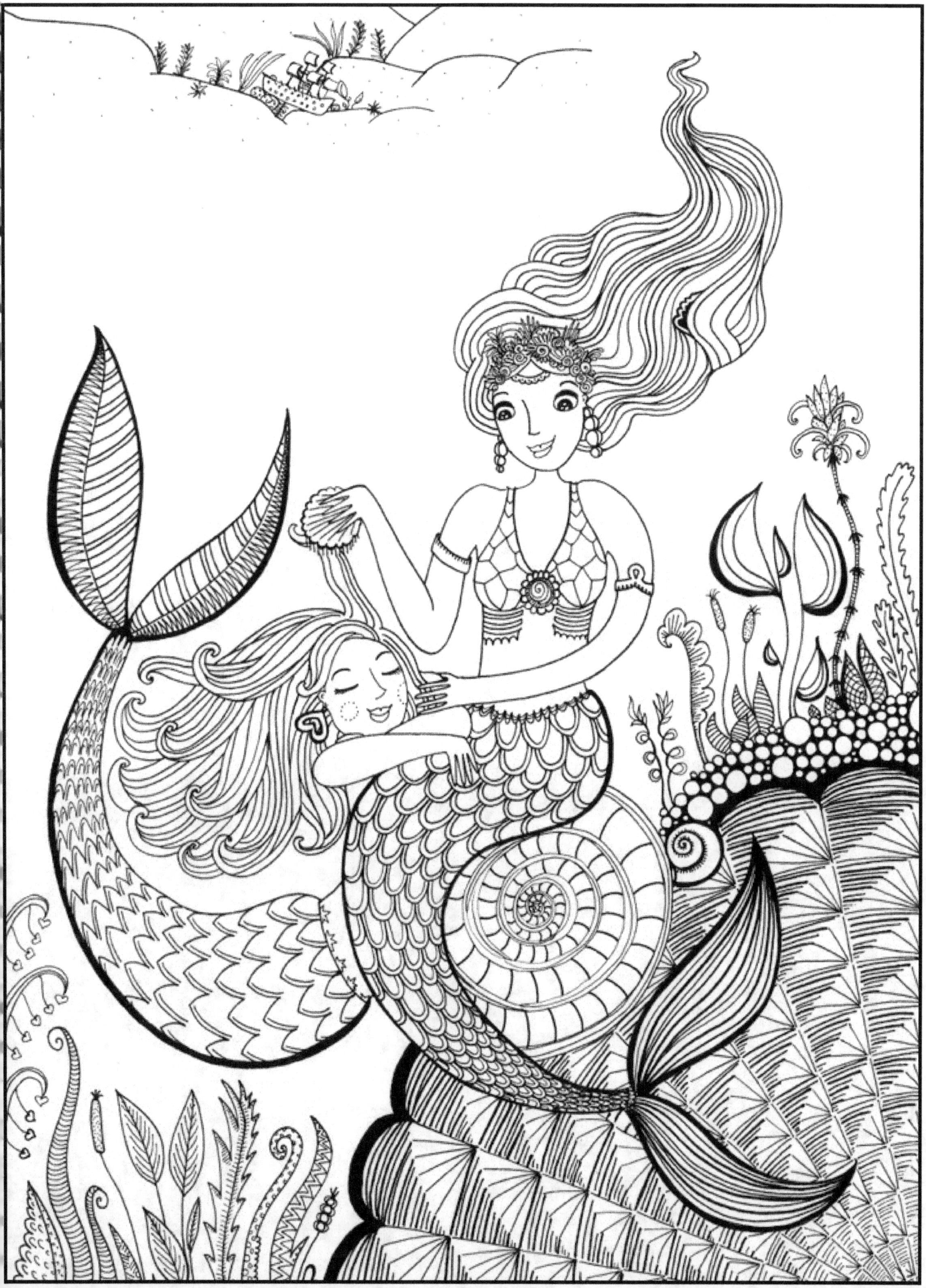

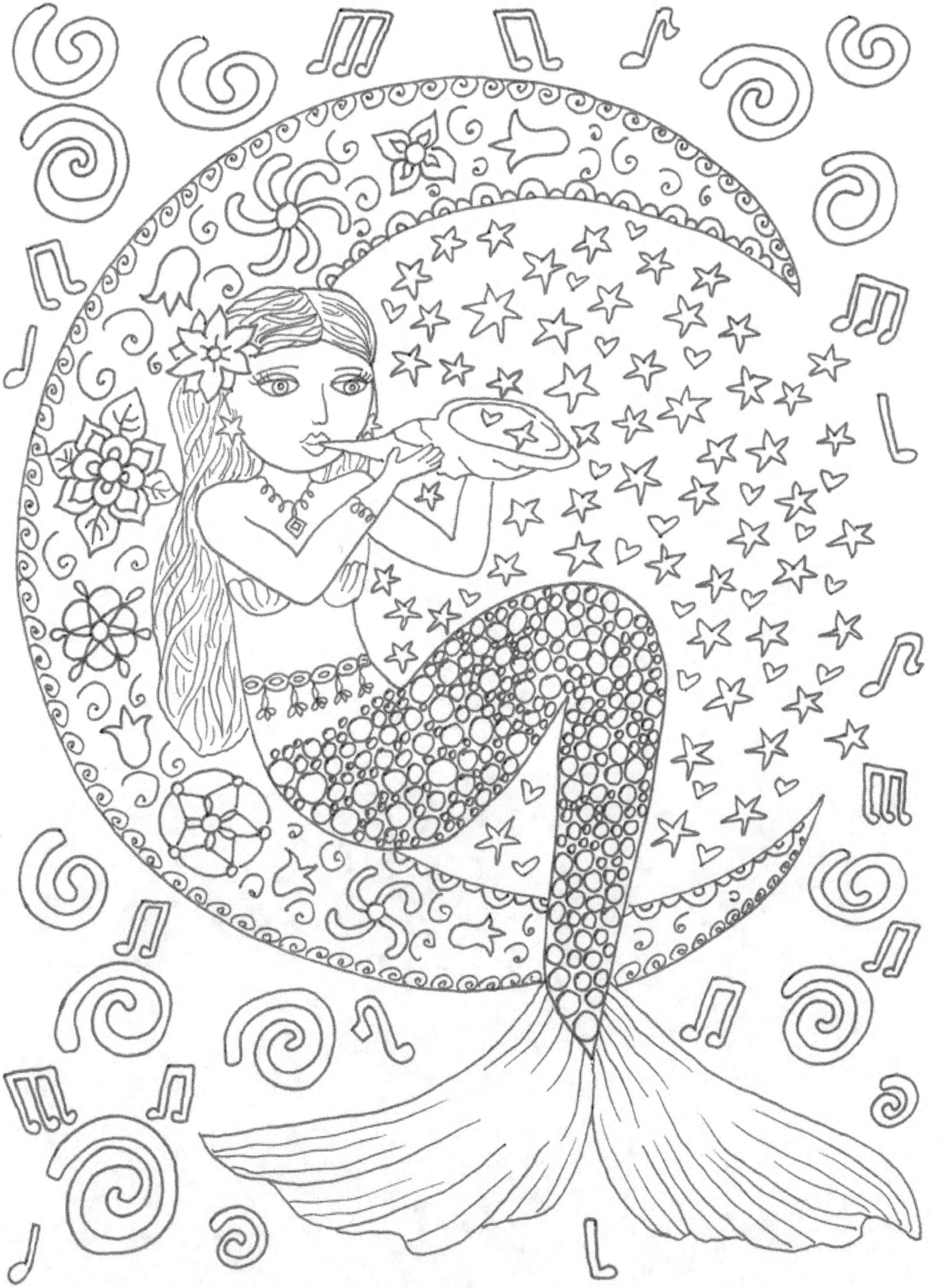

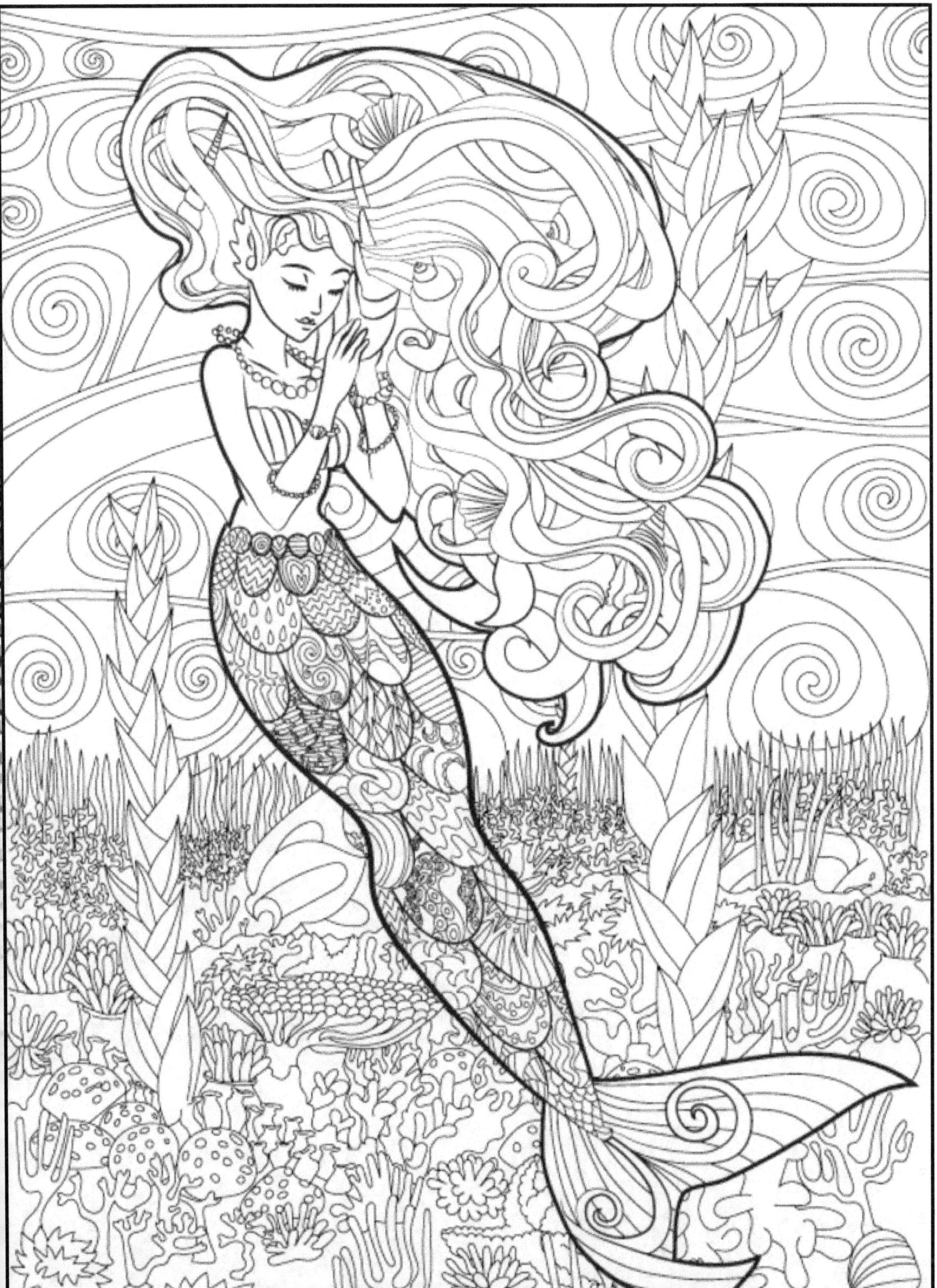

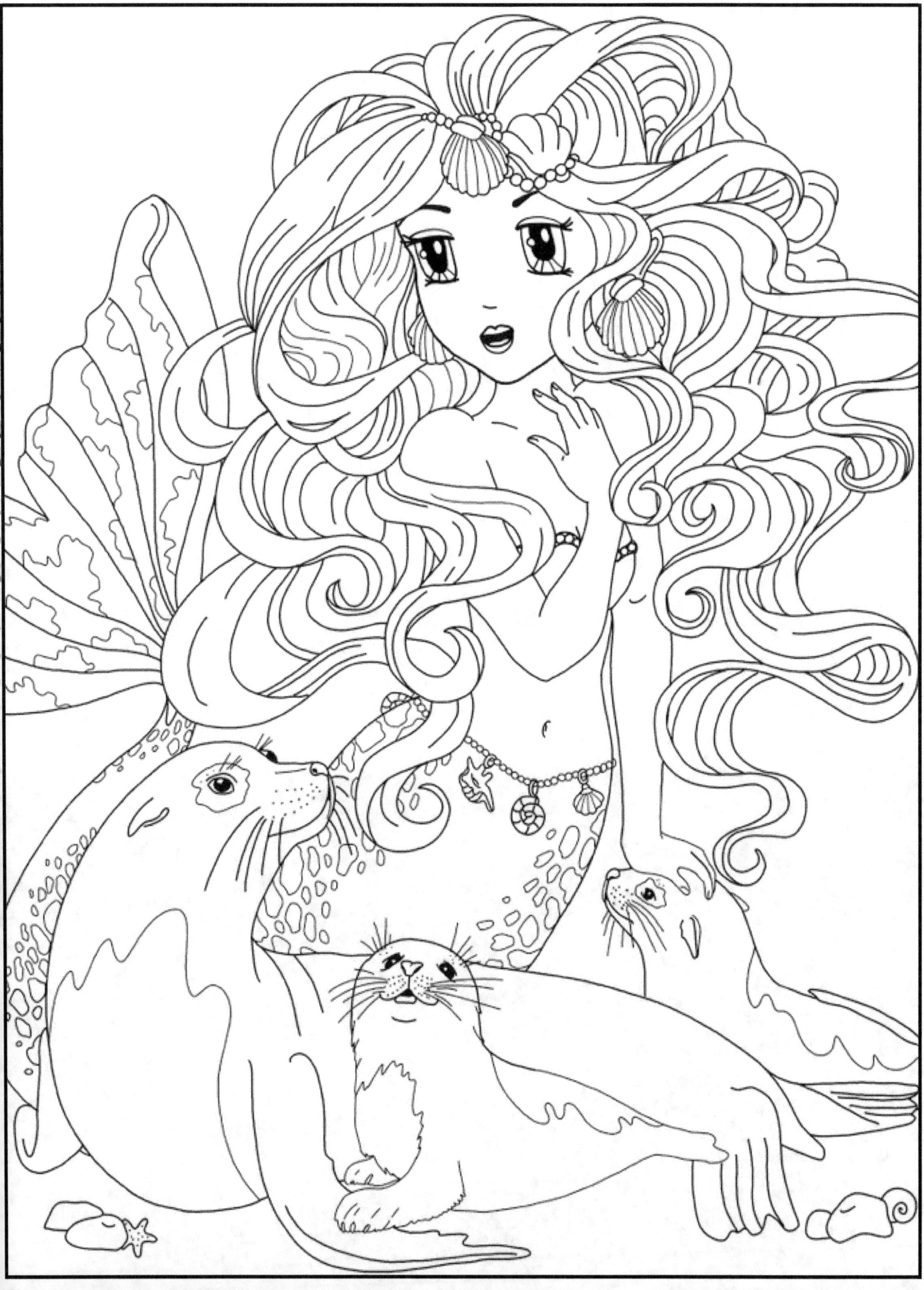

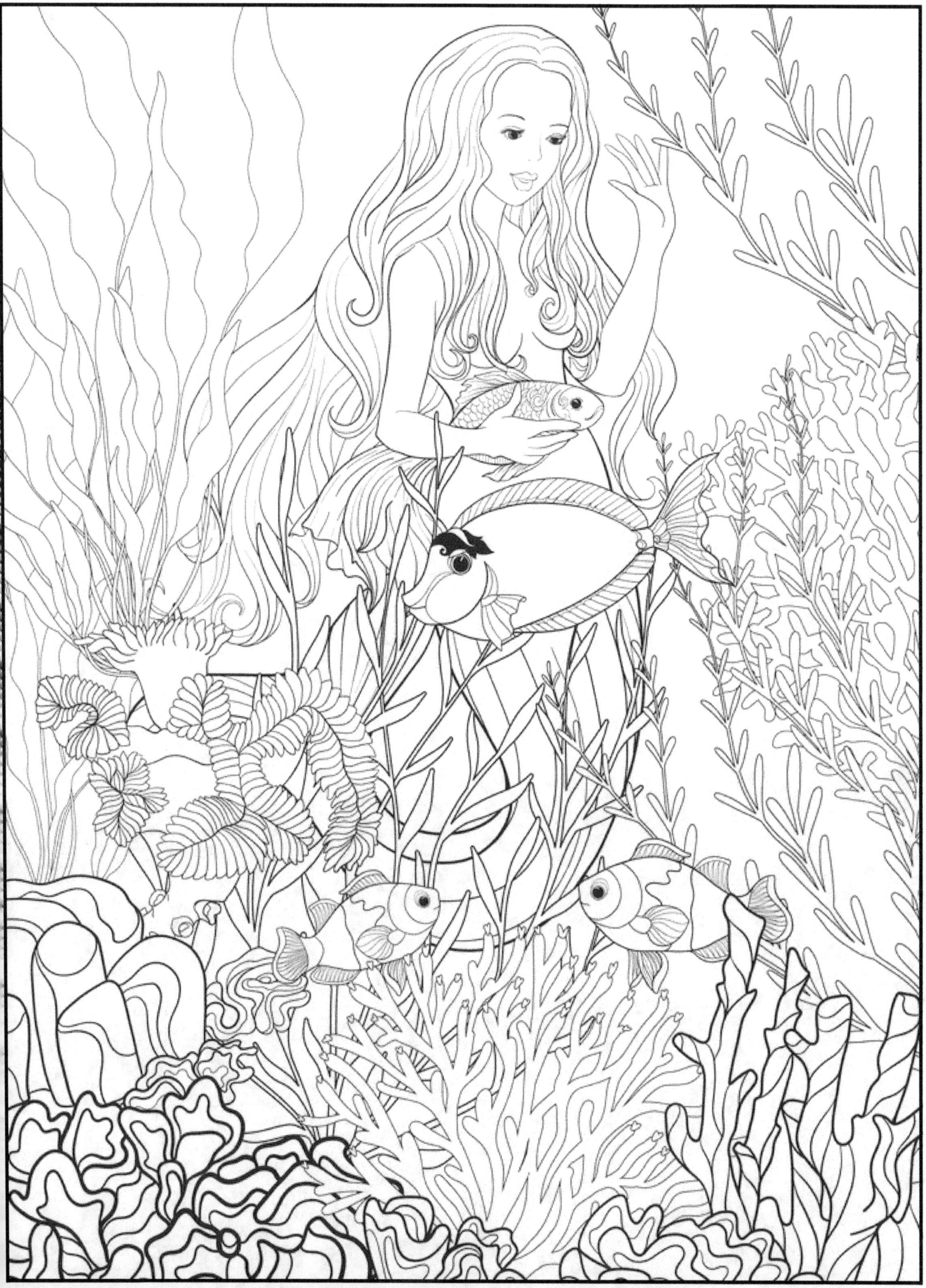

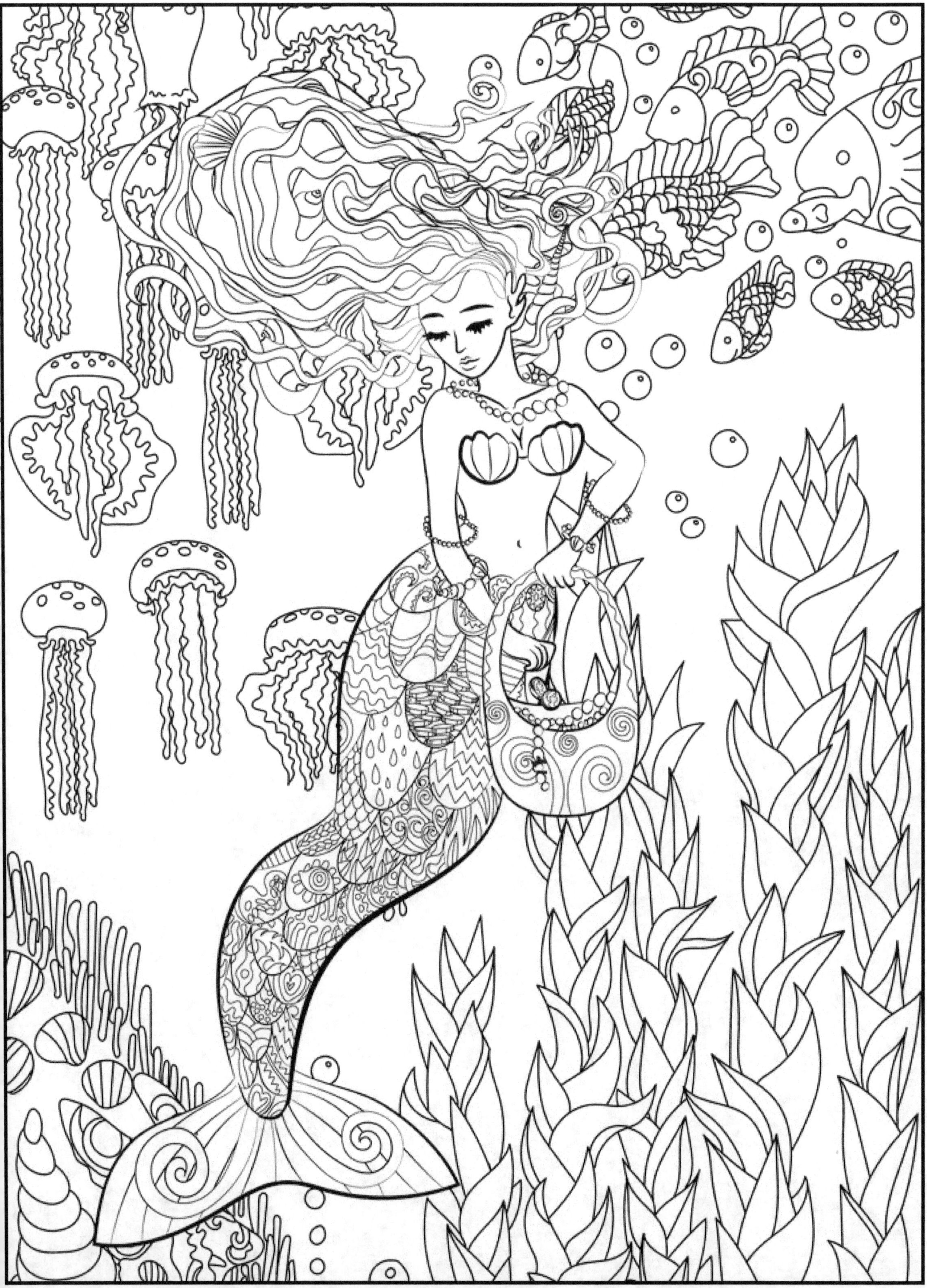

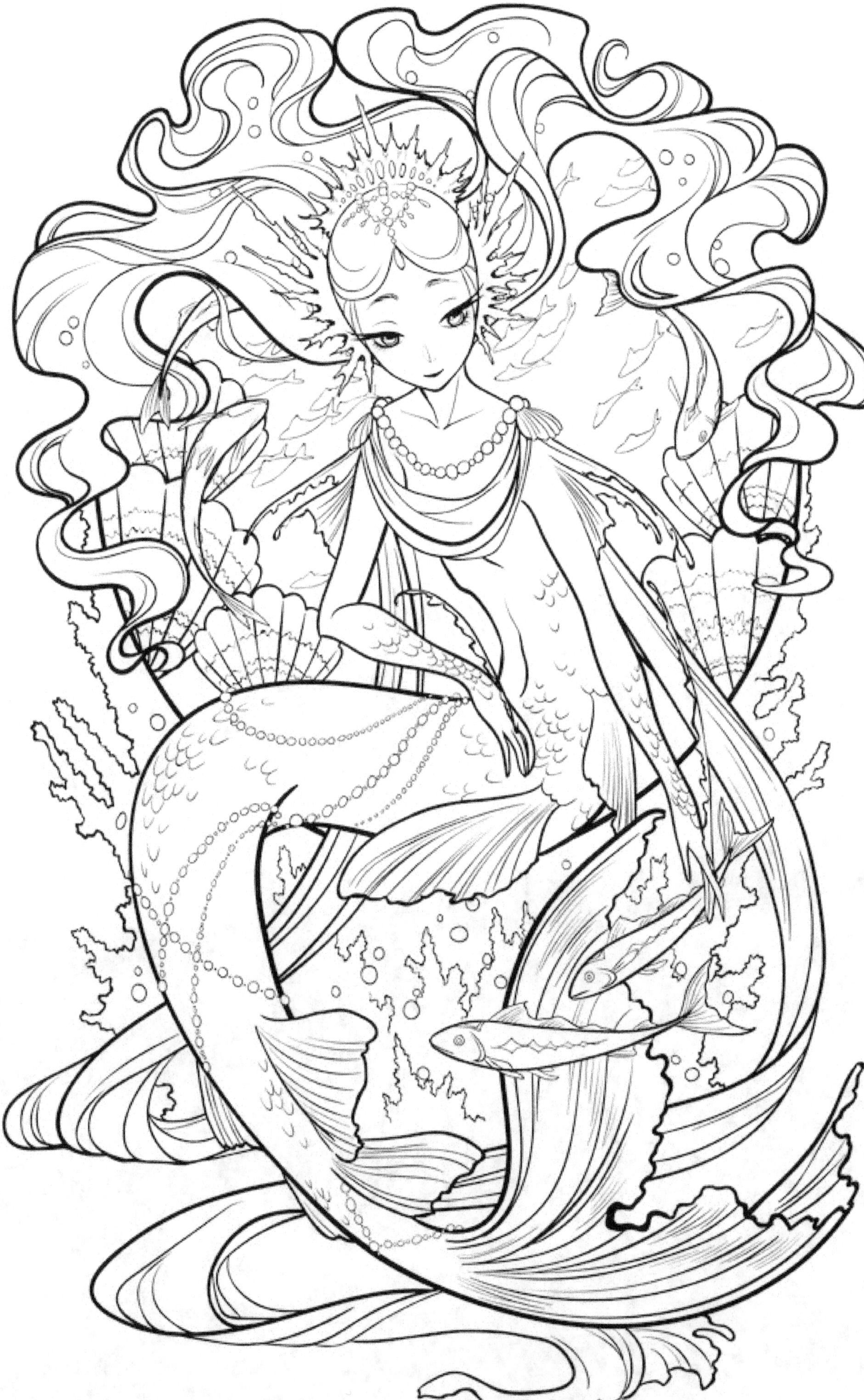

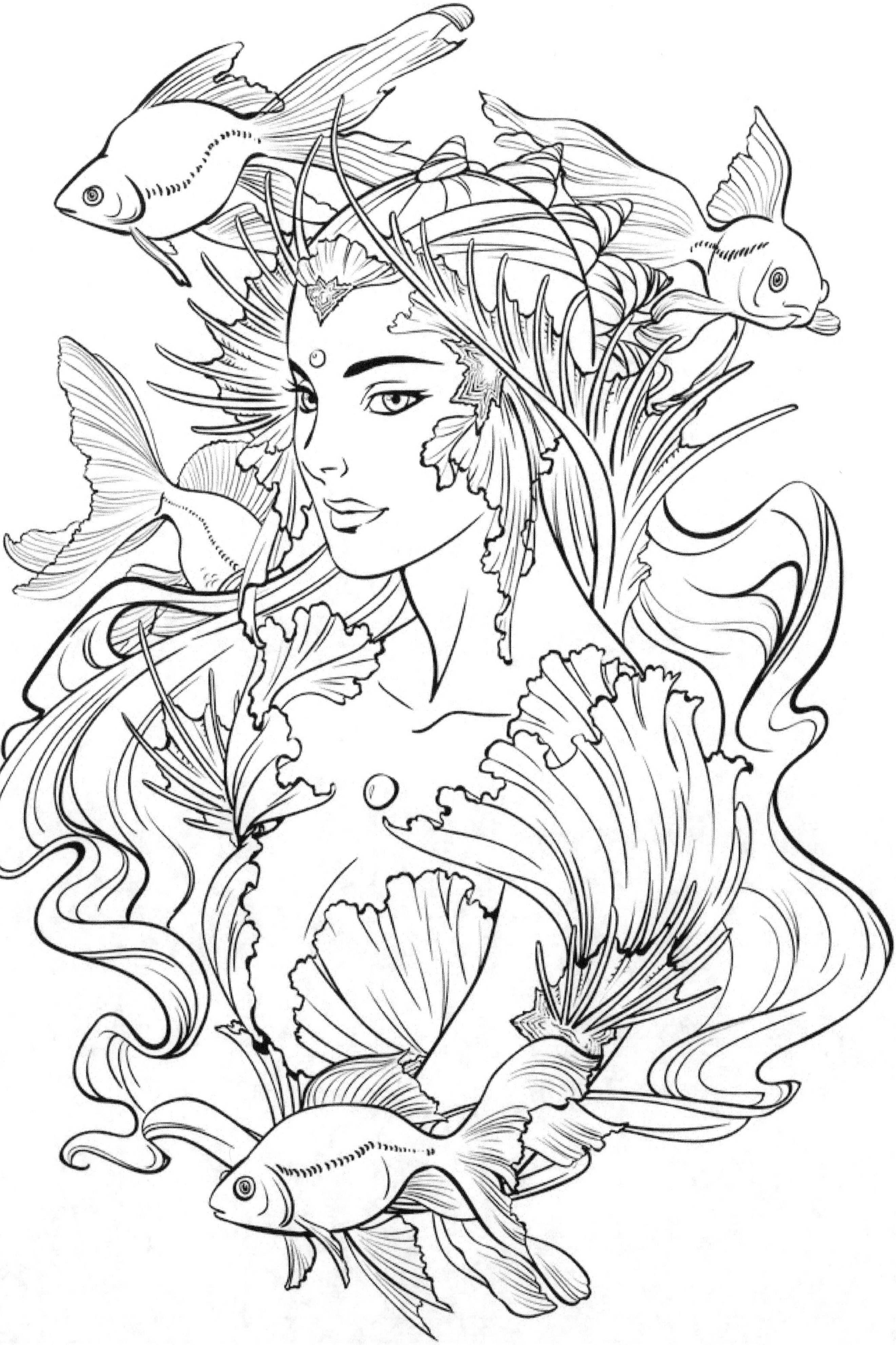

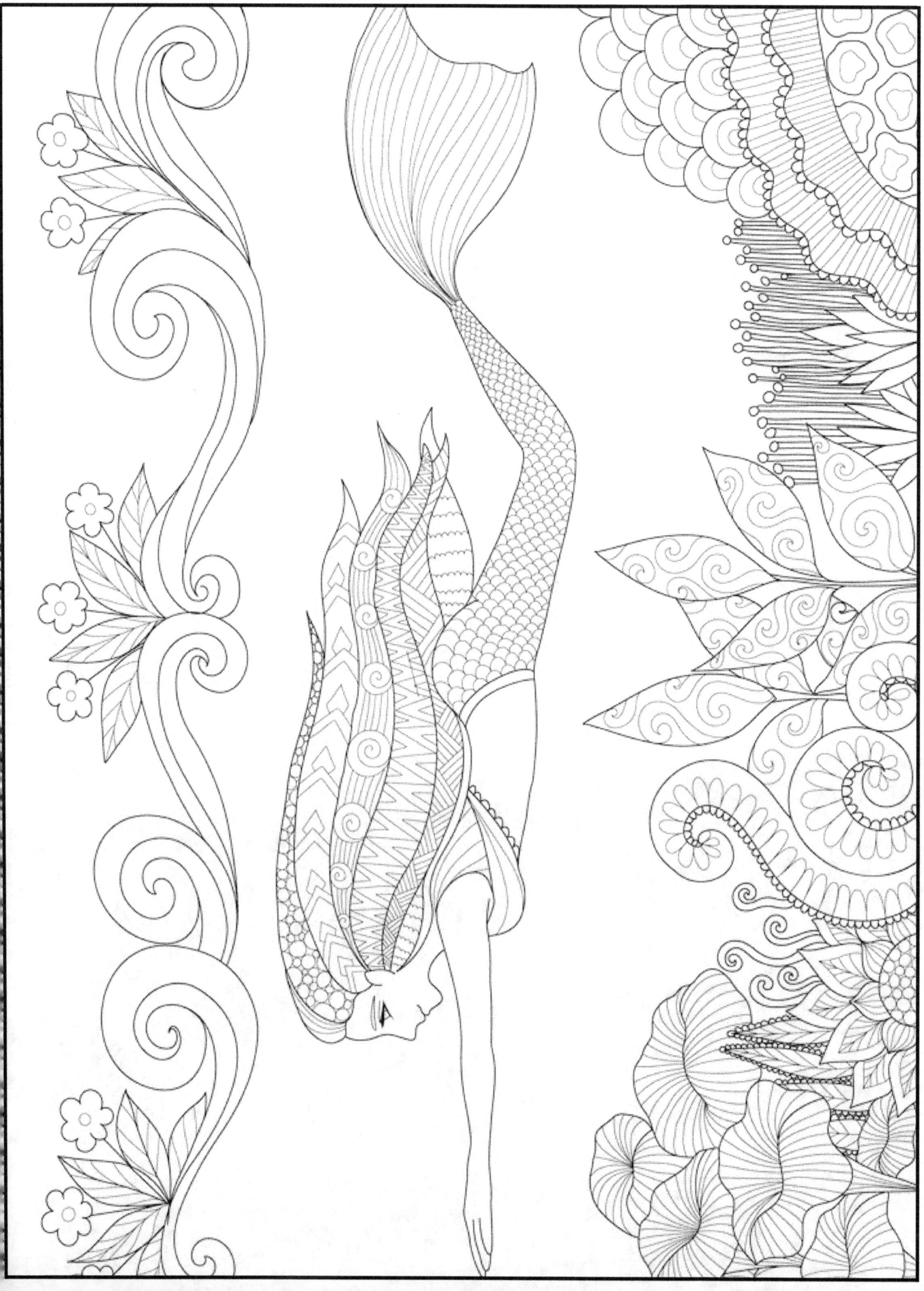

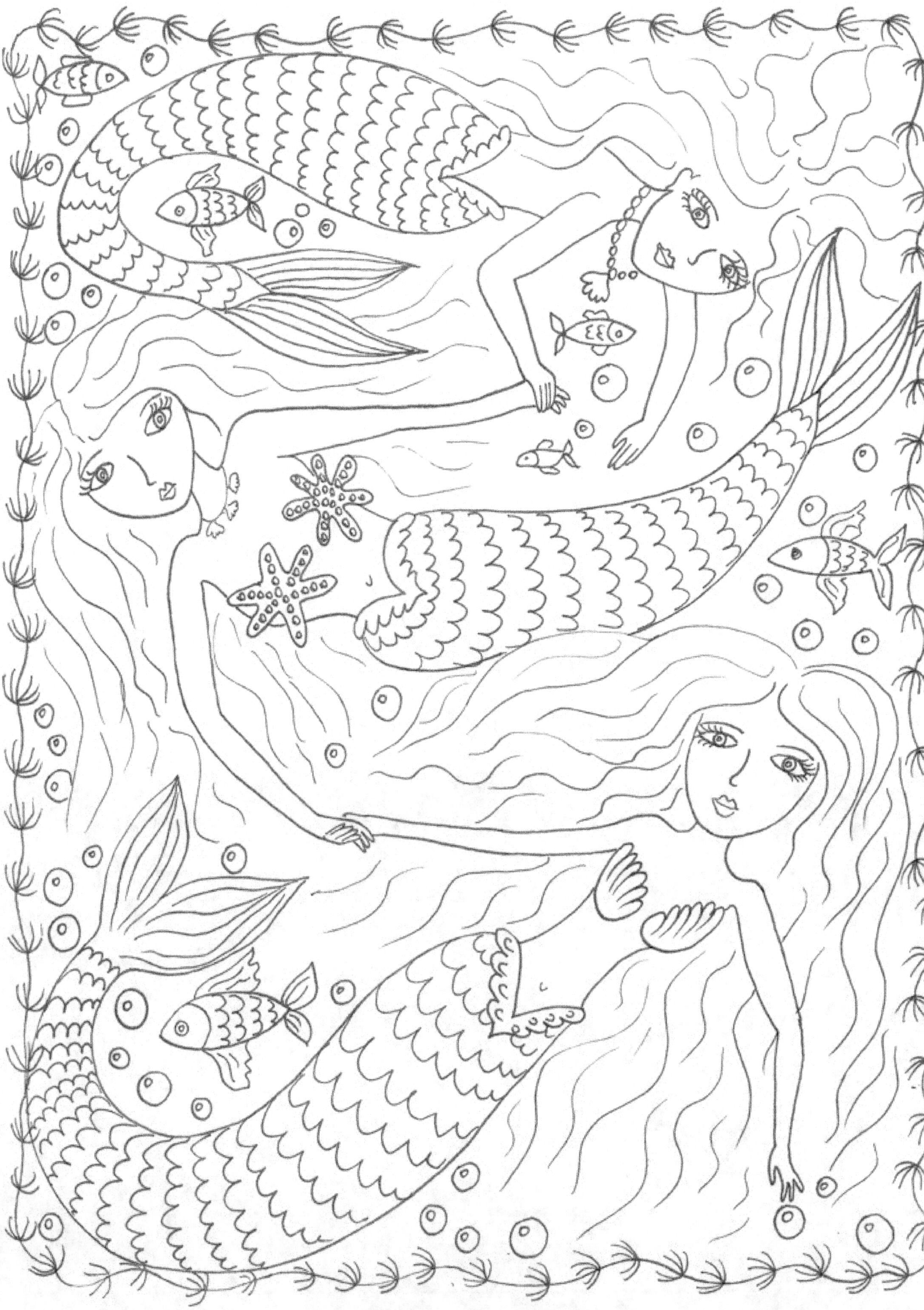

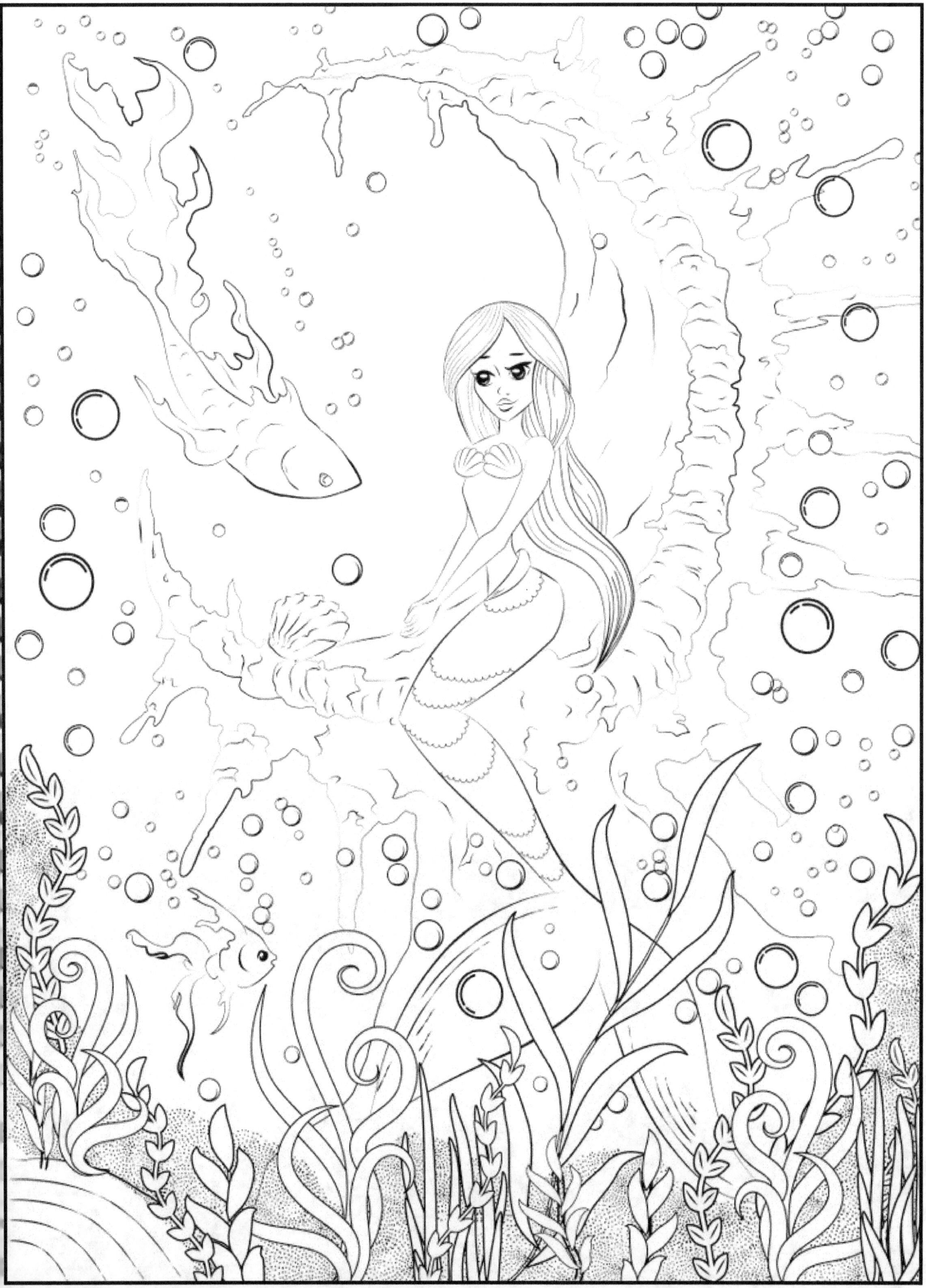

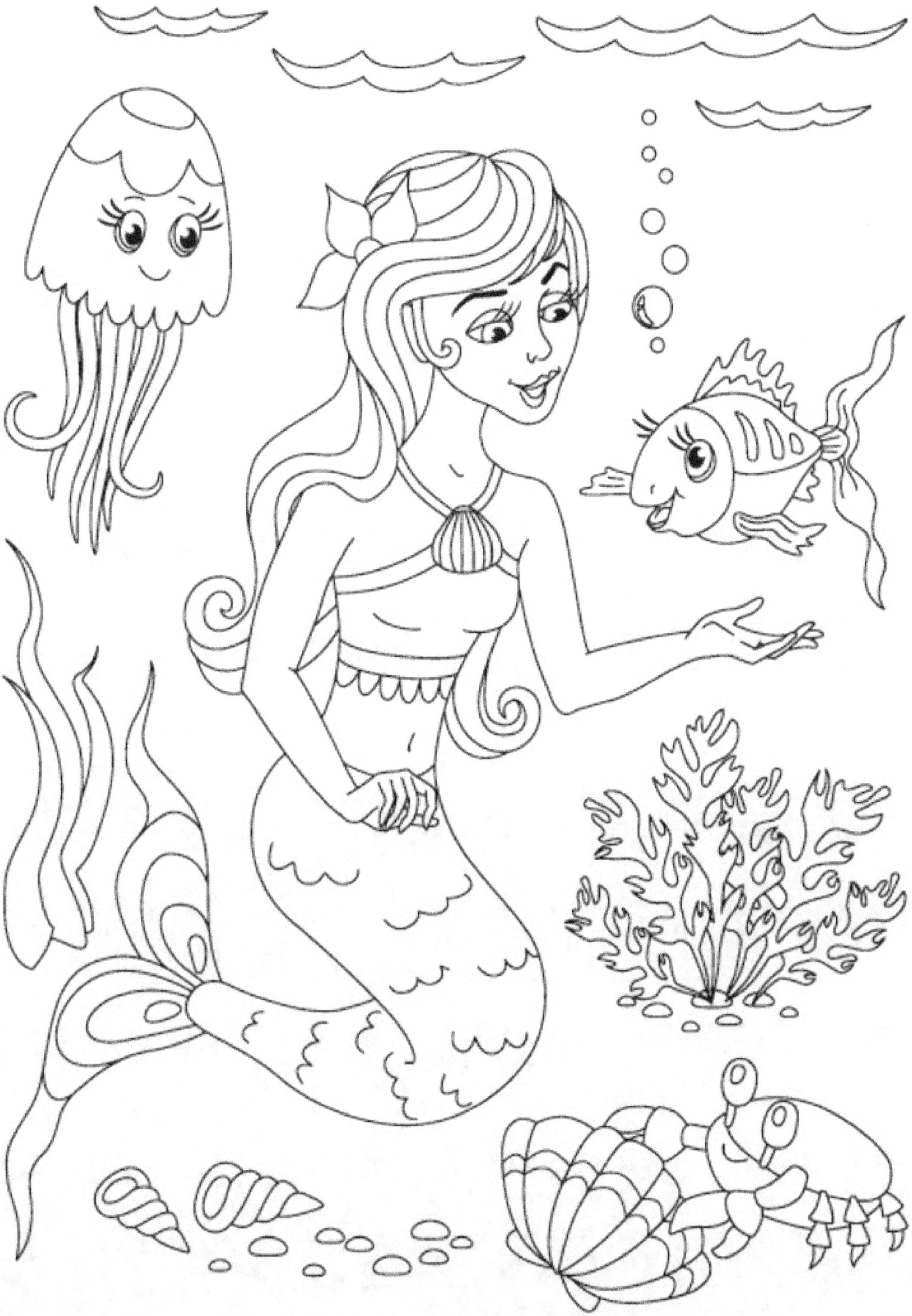

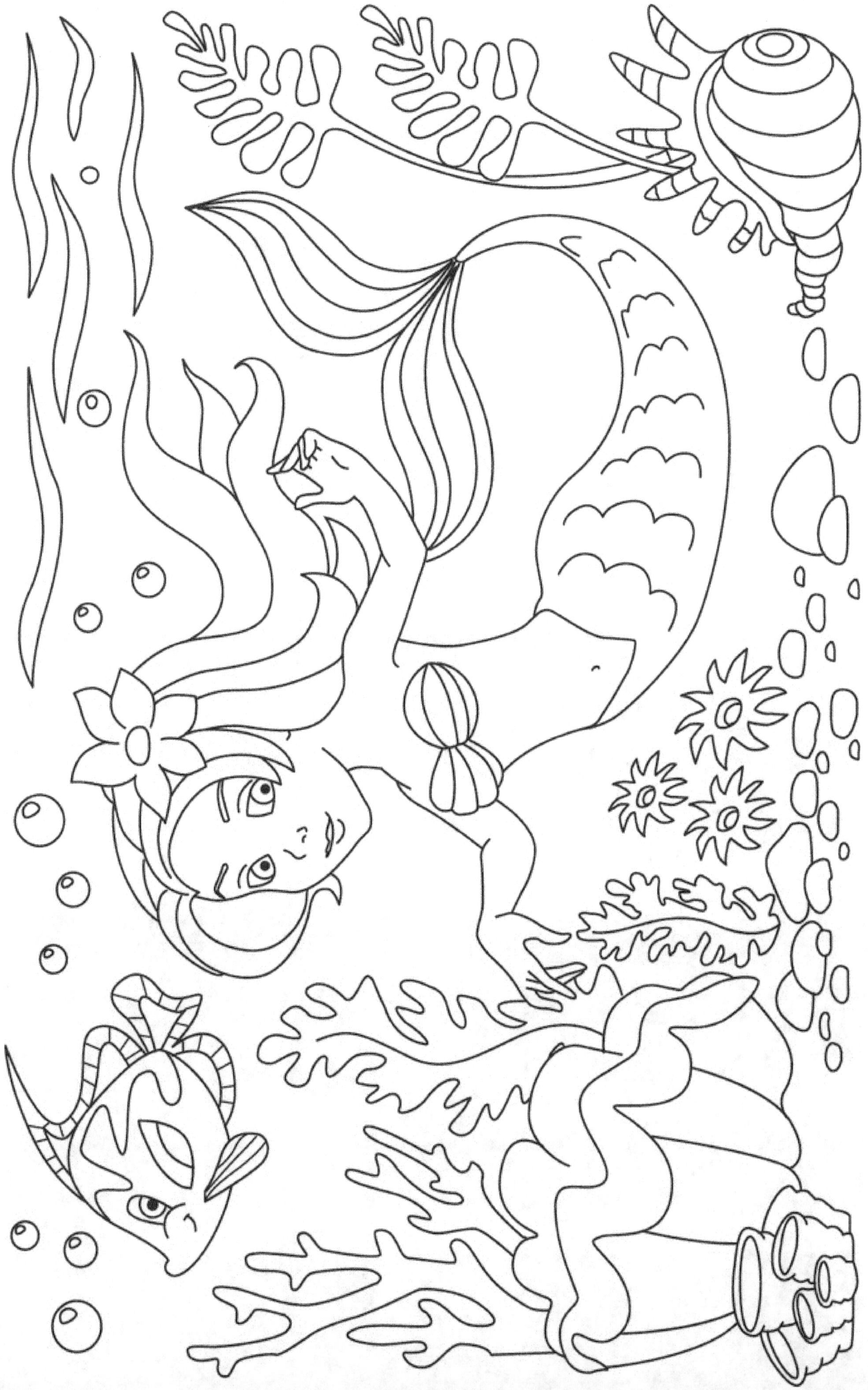

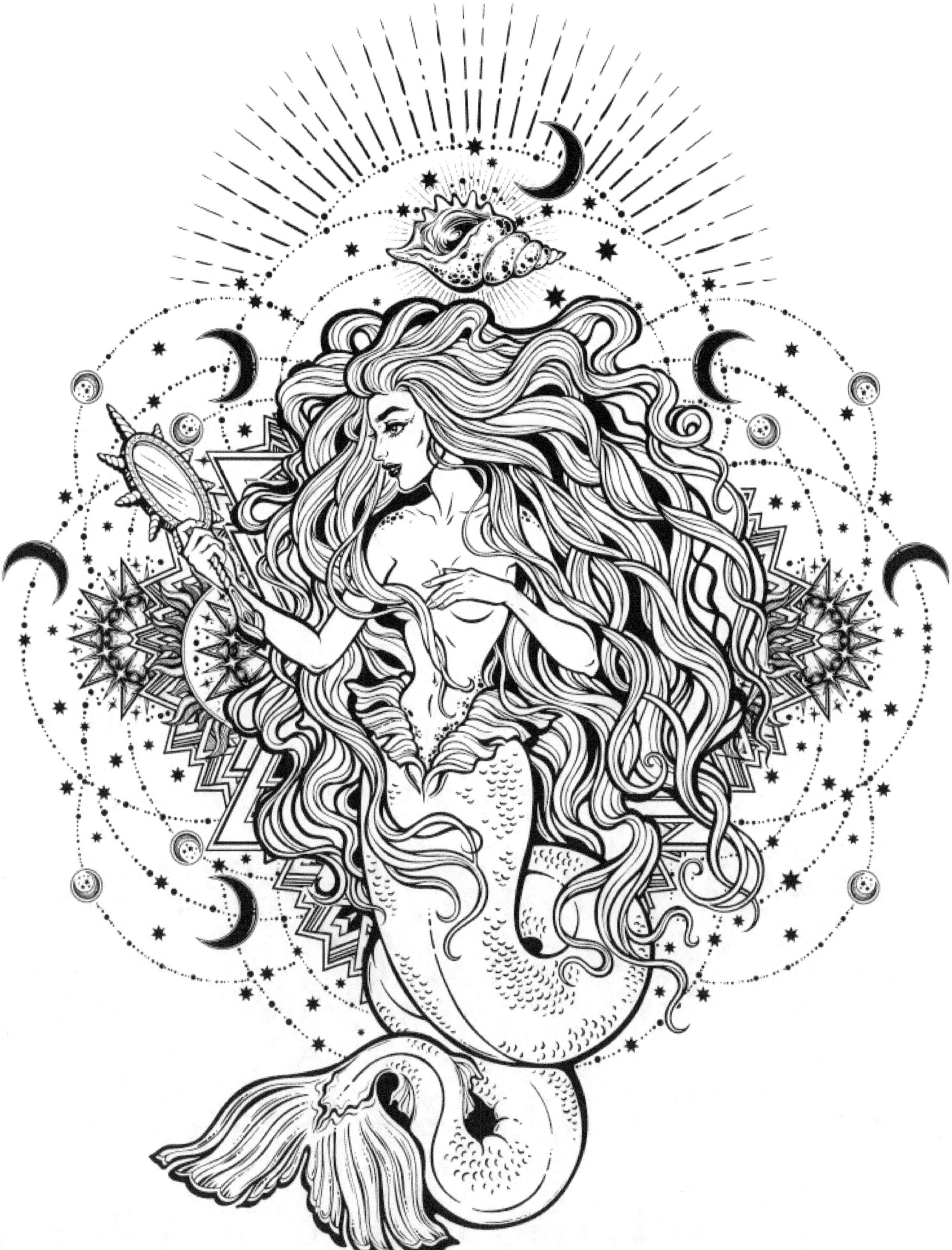

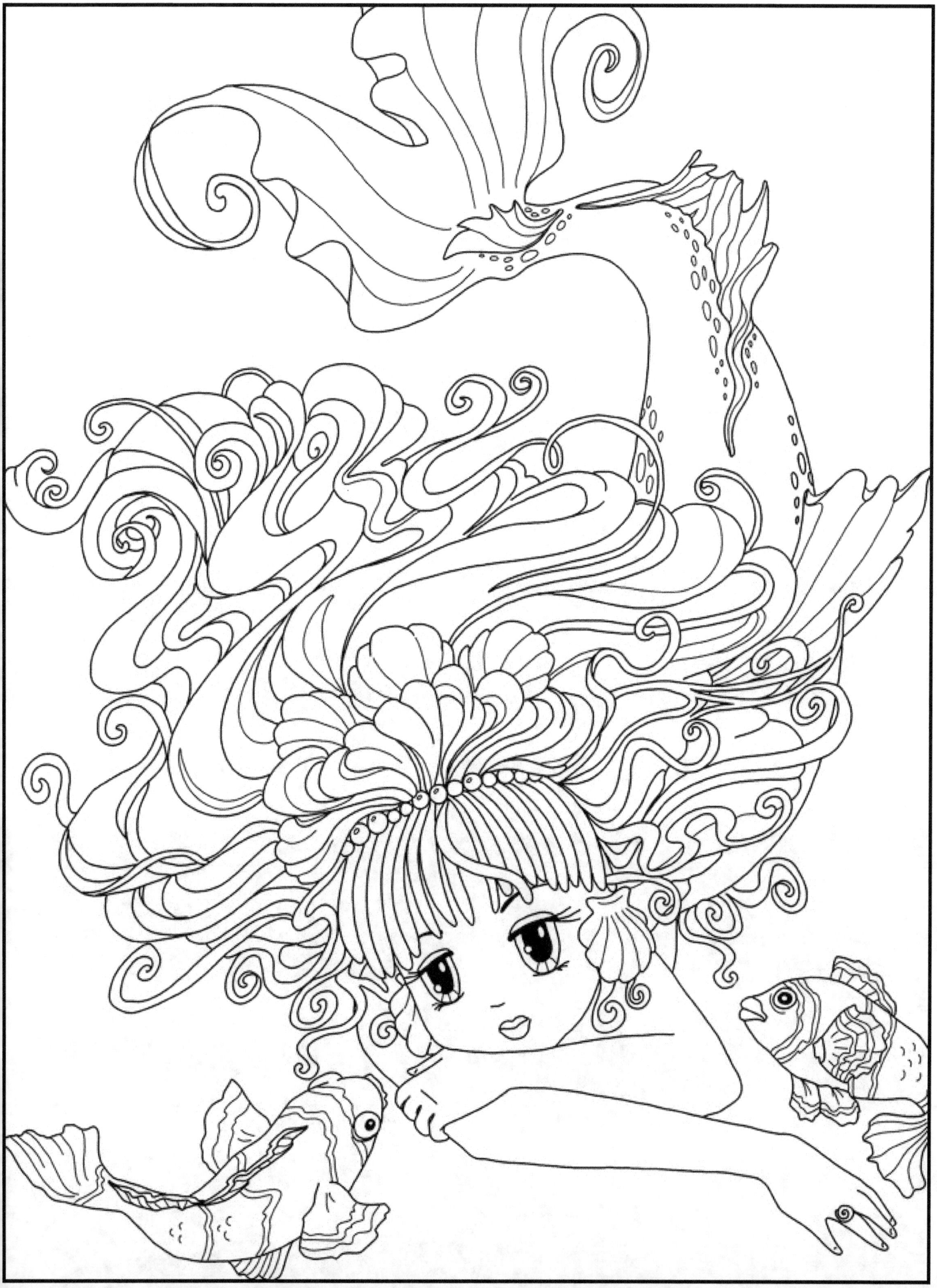

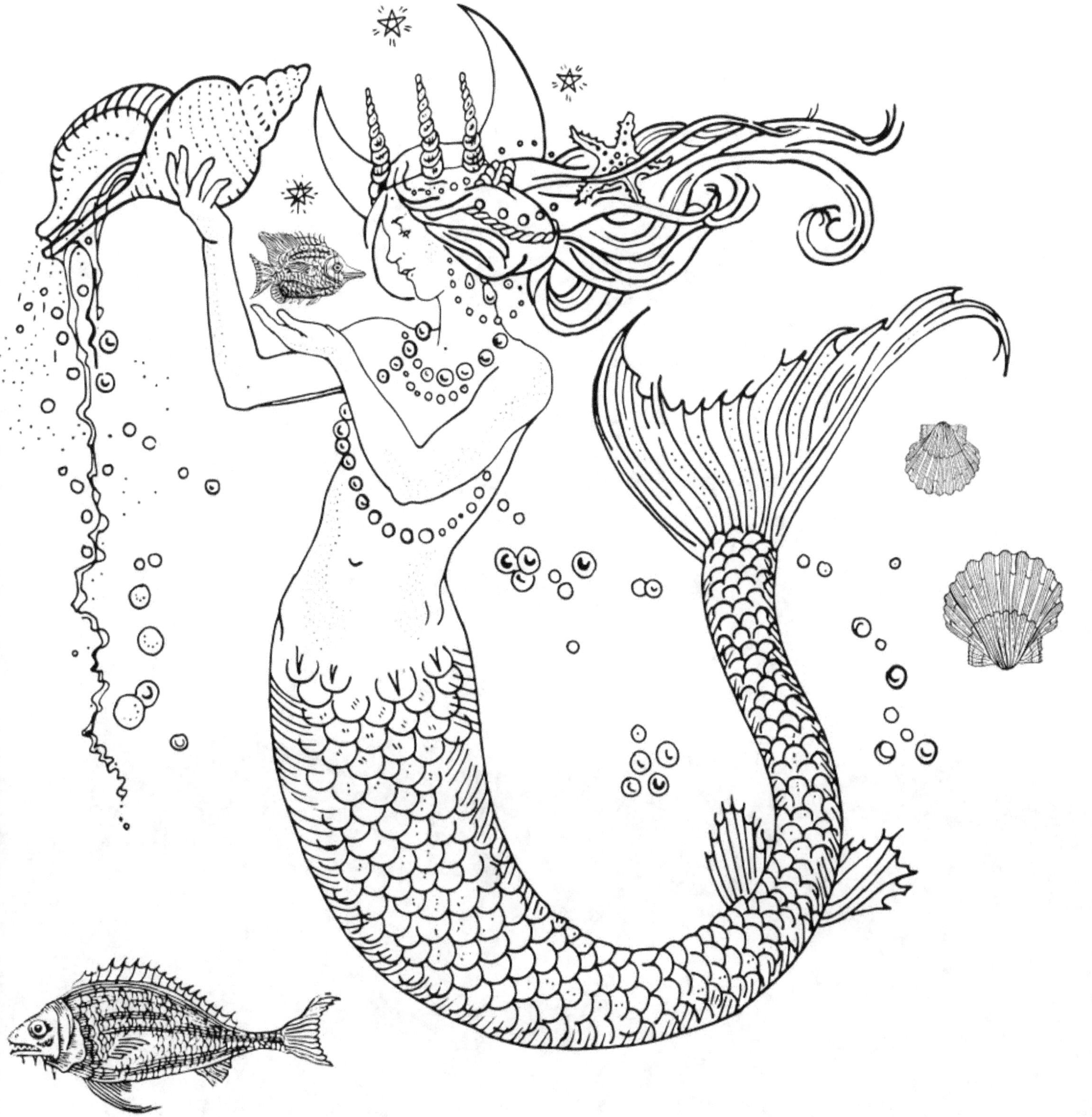

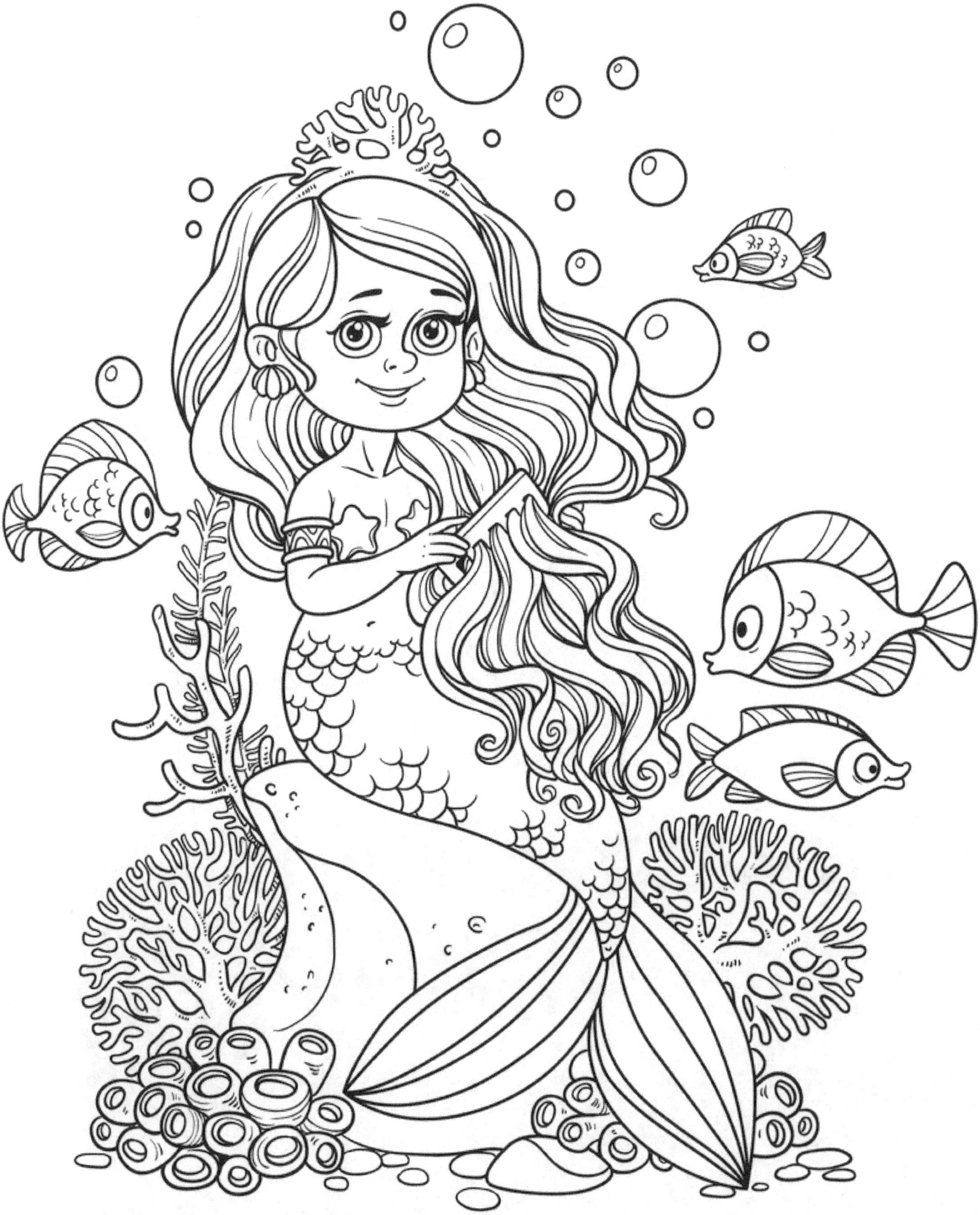

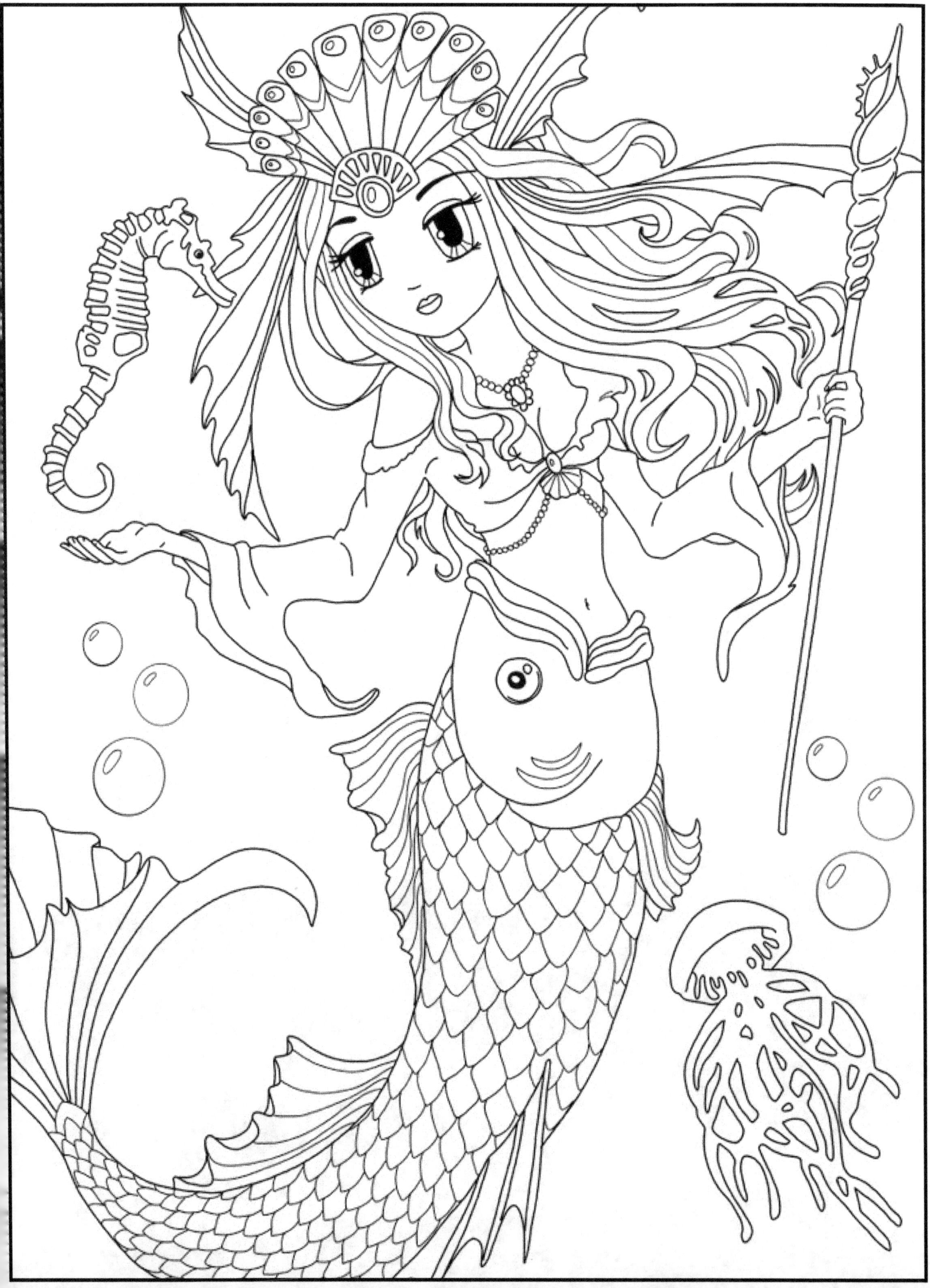

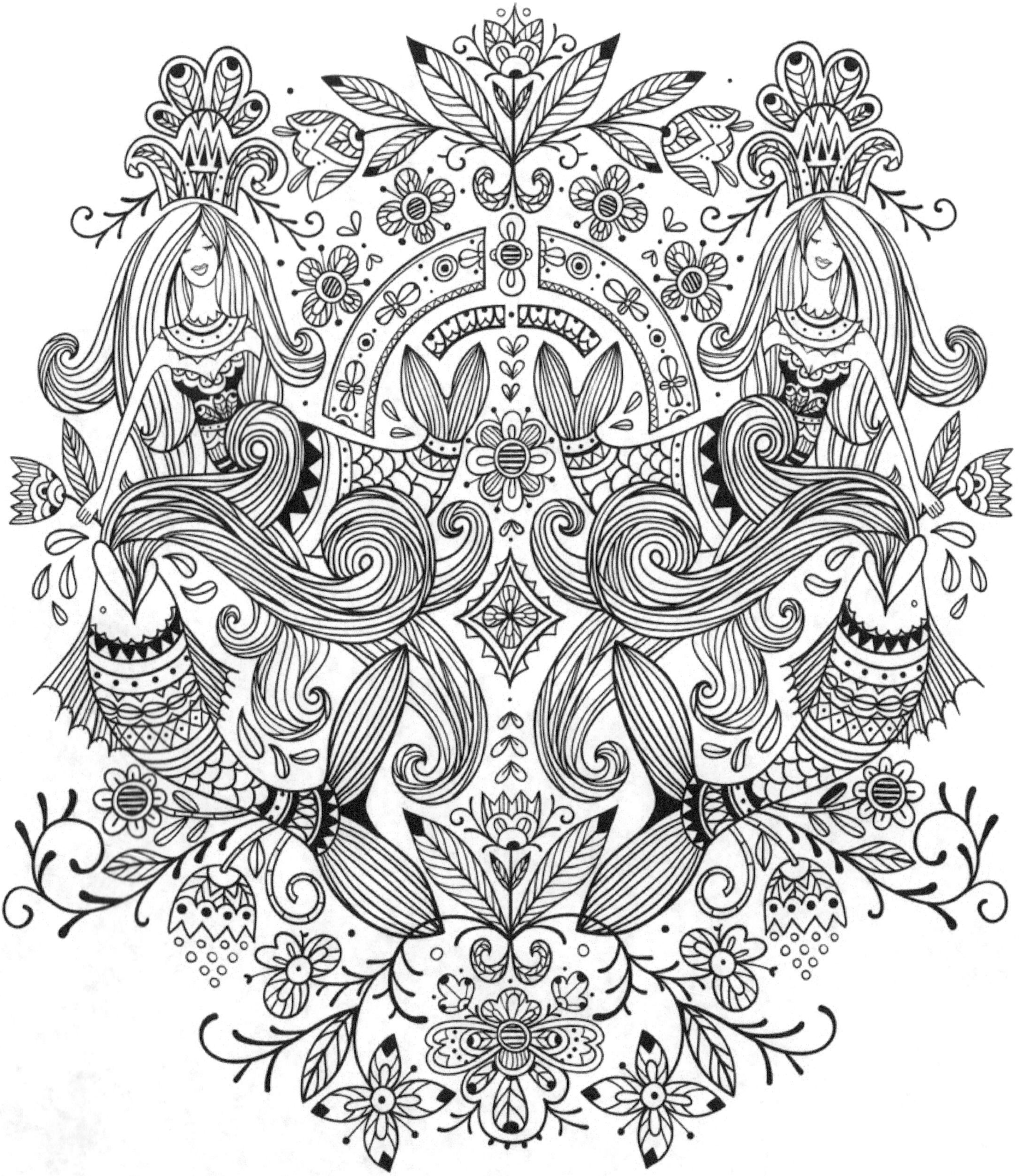

www.ingramcontent.com/pod-product-compliance
Lightning Source LLC
Chambersburg PA
CBHW080941170526
45158CB00008B/2338
* 9 7 8 1 0 7 6 7 8 5 5 3 4 *